AF251097

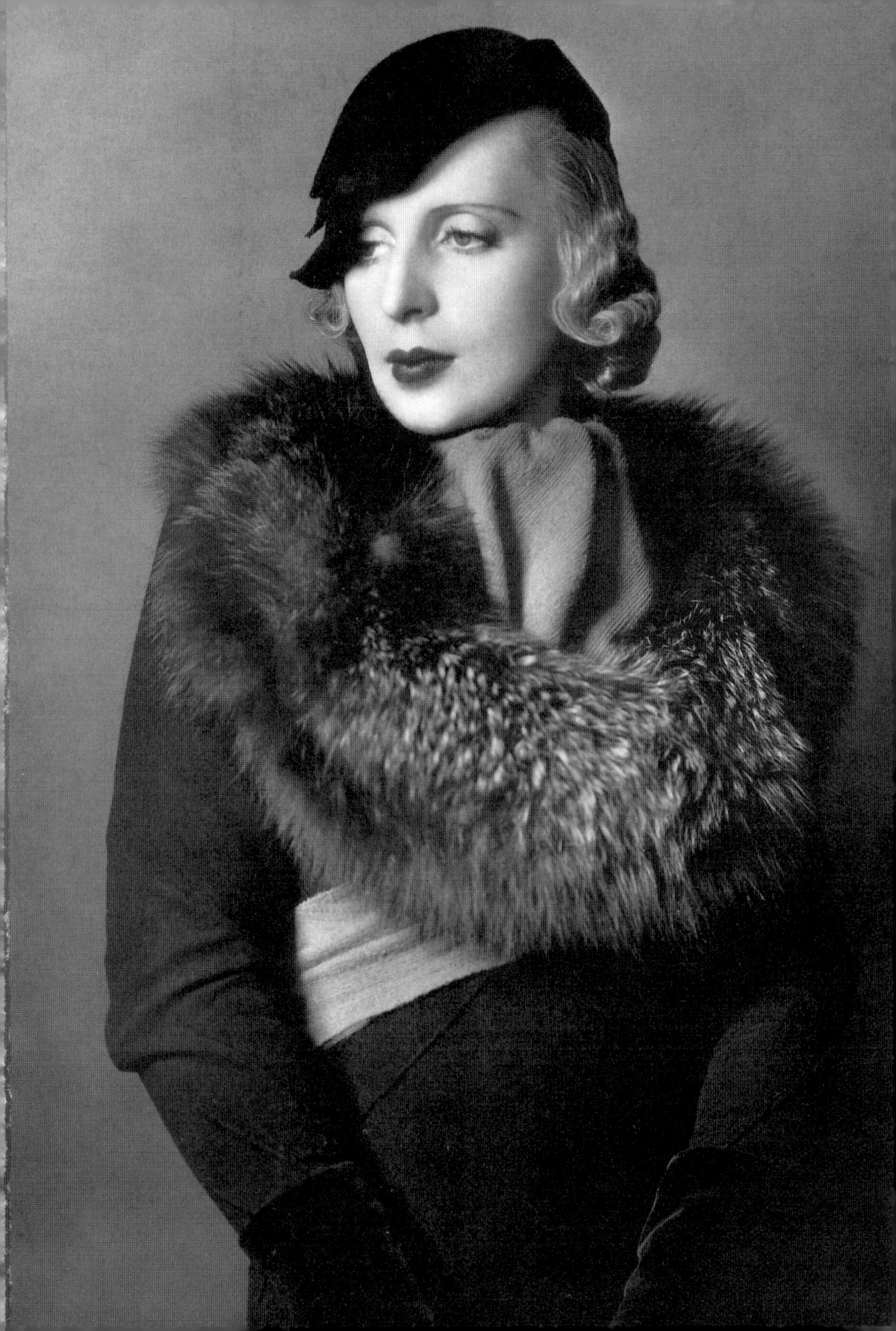

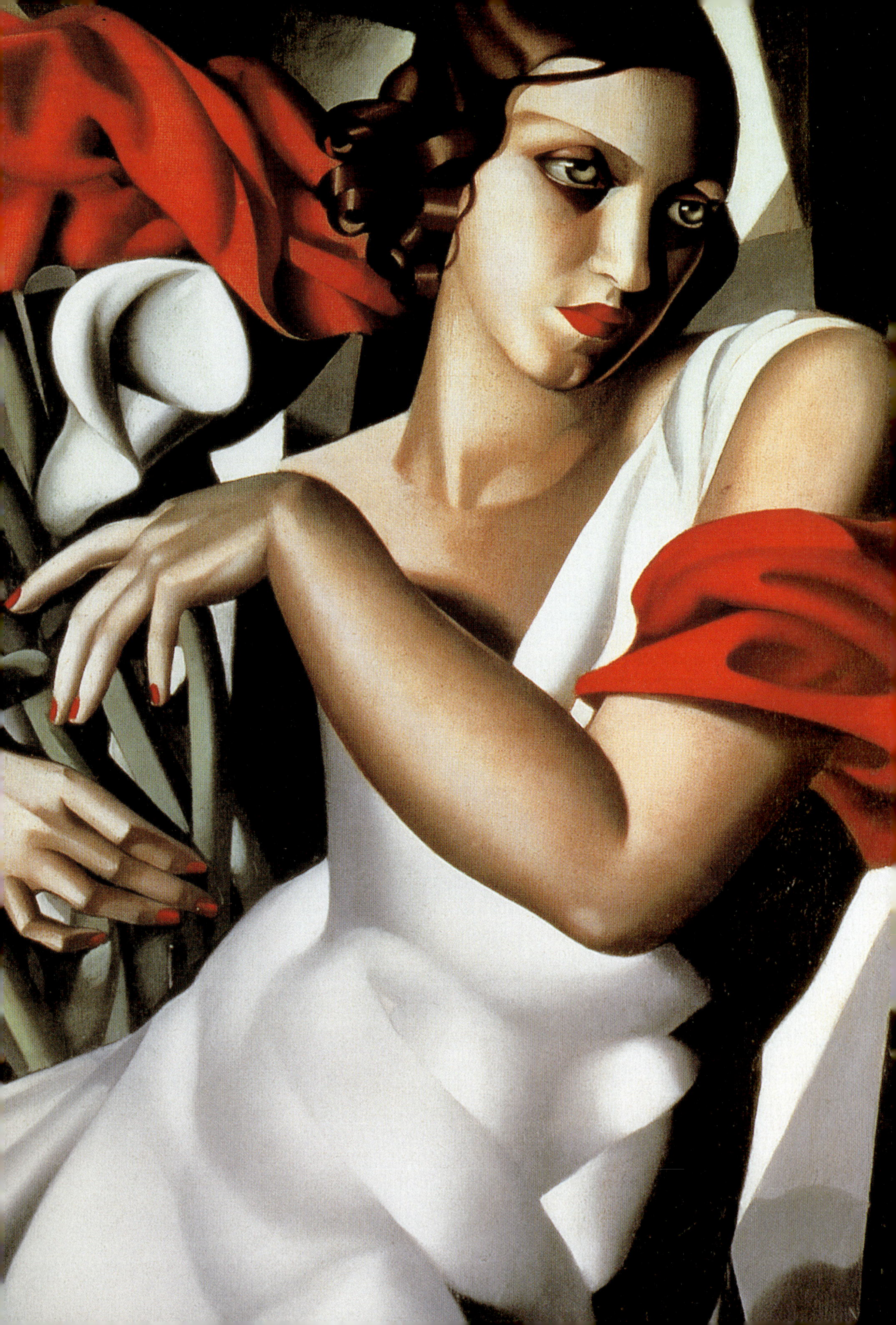

Stefanie Penck

TAMARA DE LEMPICKA

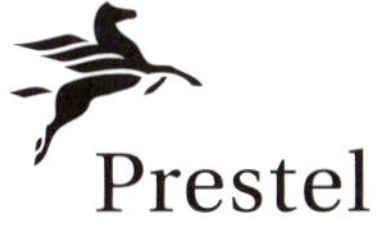

Prestel

Munich · Berlin · London · New York

Front cover: *Young Girl in Green, c.* 1927, oil on wood, 61.5 x 45.5 cm,
Musée national d'art moderne, Paris
Page 1: Dora Kallmus (photographer for the women's magazine
'Die Dame'), Tamara de Lempicka with hat and fox fur, *c.* 1929
Page 2: *Portrait of Ira P.,* see pages 54/55
Spine: *Woman in a Black Dress* (detail), 1923, see page 17
Back cover: *Self-Portrait (Tamara in the Green Bugatti),* 1929, see page 60

The Library of Congress Cataloguing-in-Publication data is available;
British Library Cataloguing-in-Publication Data: a catalogue record for
this book is available from the British Library; Deutsche Bibliothek holds
a record of this publication in the Deutsche Nationalbibliografie; detailed
bibliographical data can be found under: http://dnb.ddb.de

Photographic Credits: pp. 24, 34, 37, 59, 61: akg-images, Berlin;
p. 47: Christie's-Artothek; cover, p. 63: The Bridgeman Art Library, London;
pp. 30, 54, 67: RMN Paris; pp. 17, 41, 57, 65, 89; Wolfgang Joop Collection
(wunderkind.art), Potsdam; pp. 1, 23, 25, 26 (centre and bottom), 27,
31 (top), 32 (top and centre): from Alain Blondel, *Lempicka*, catalogue
raisonné, Lausanne, 1999

Prestel books are available worldwide. Please contact your nearest
bookseller or one of the following Prestel offices for information
concerning your local distributor:

Prestel Verlag
Königinstrasse 9, 80539 Munich
Tel. +49 (89) 38 17 09-0; Fax +49 (89) 38 17 09-35

Prestel Publishing Ltd.
4 Bloomsbury Place, London WC1A 2QA
Tel. +44 (020) 7323-5004; Fax +44 (020) 7636-8004

Prestel Publishing
900 Broadway, Suite 603, New York, NY 10003
Tel. +1 (212) 995-2720; Fax +1 (212) 995-2733

www.prestel.com

Translated from the German by Ishbel Flett, Edinburgh
Copyedited by Christopher Wynne

Design and layout: Matthias Hauer
Fonts: *Utopia* and *Placard*
Origination: Reproline mediateam, Munich
Printing and binding: Appl, Wemding

Printed in Germany on acid-free paper

ISBN 3-7913-3171-X

Contents

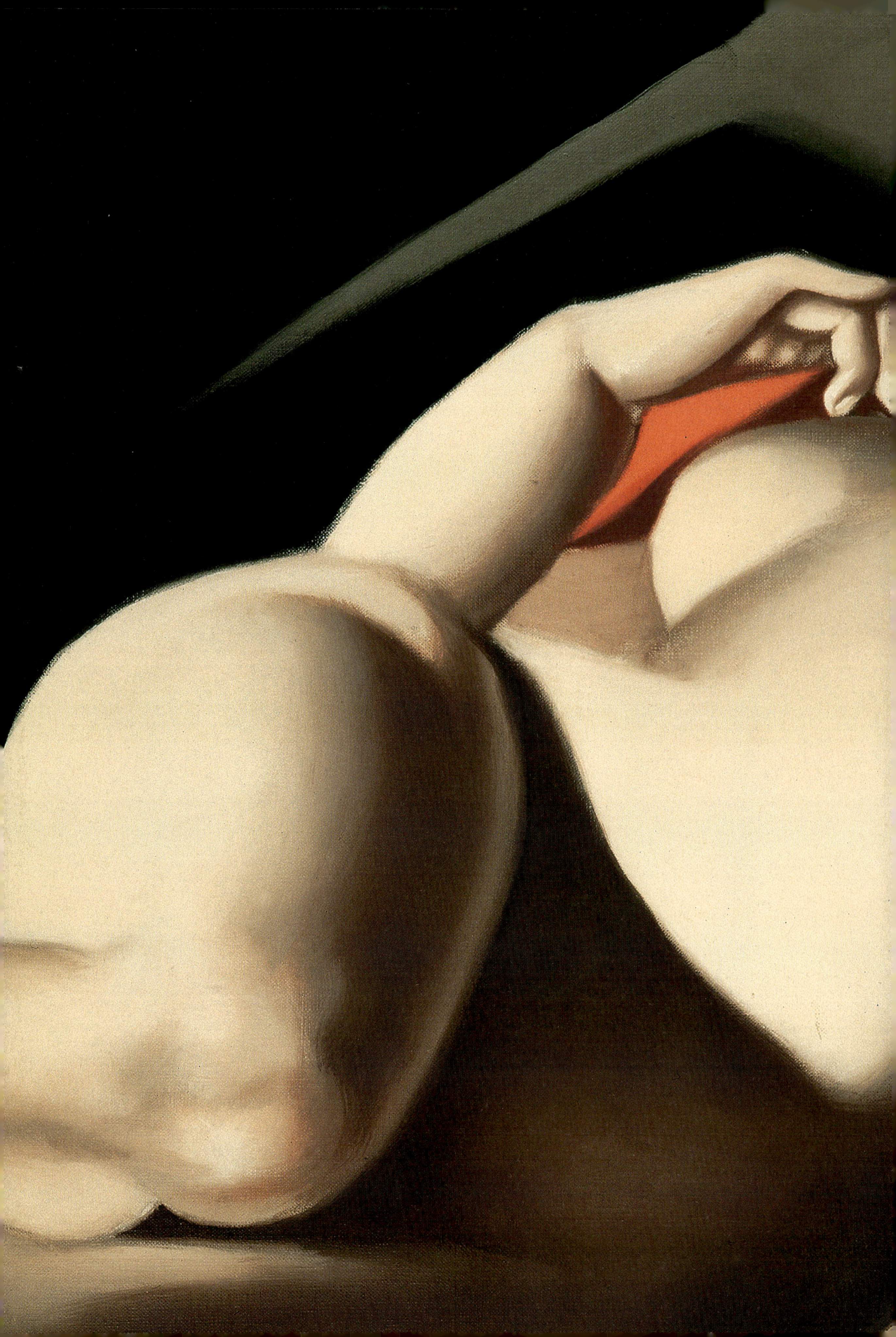

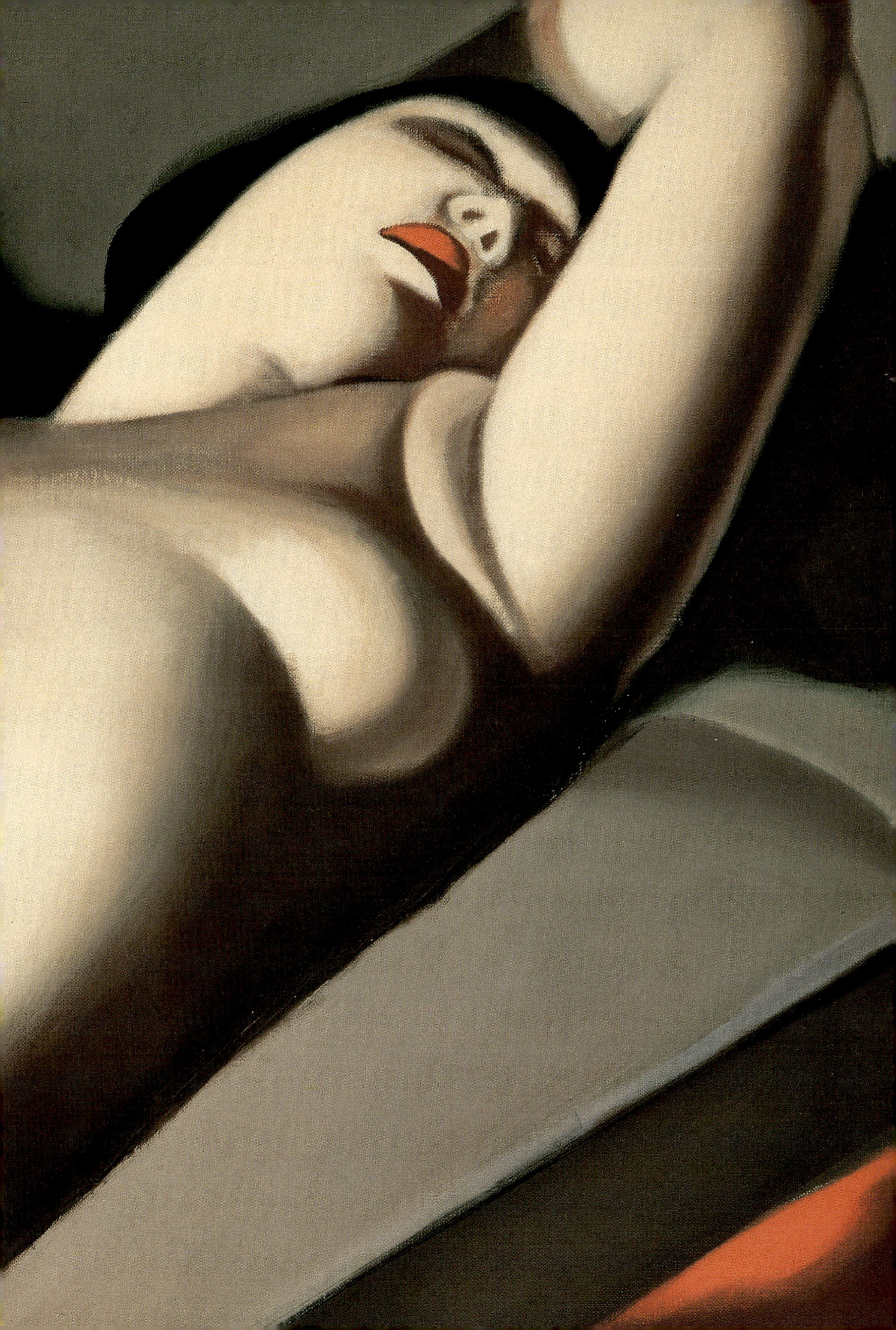

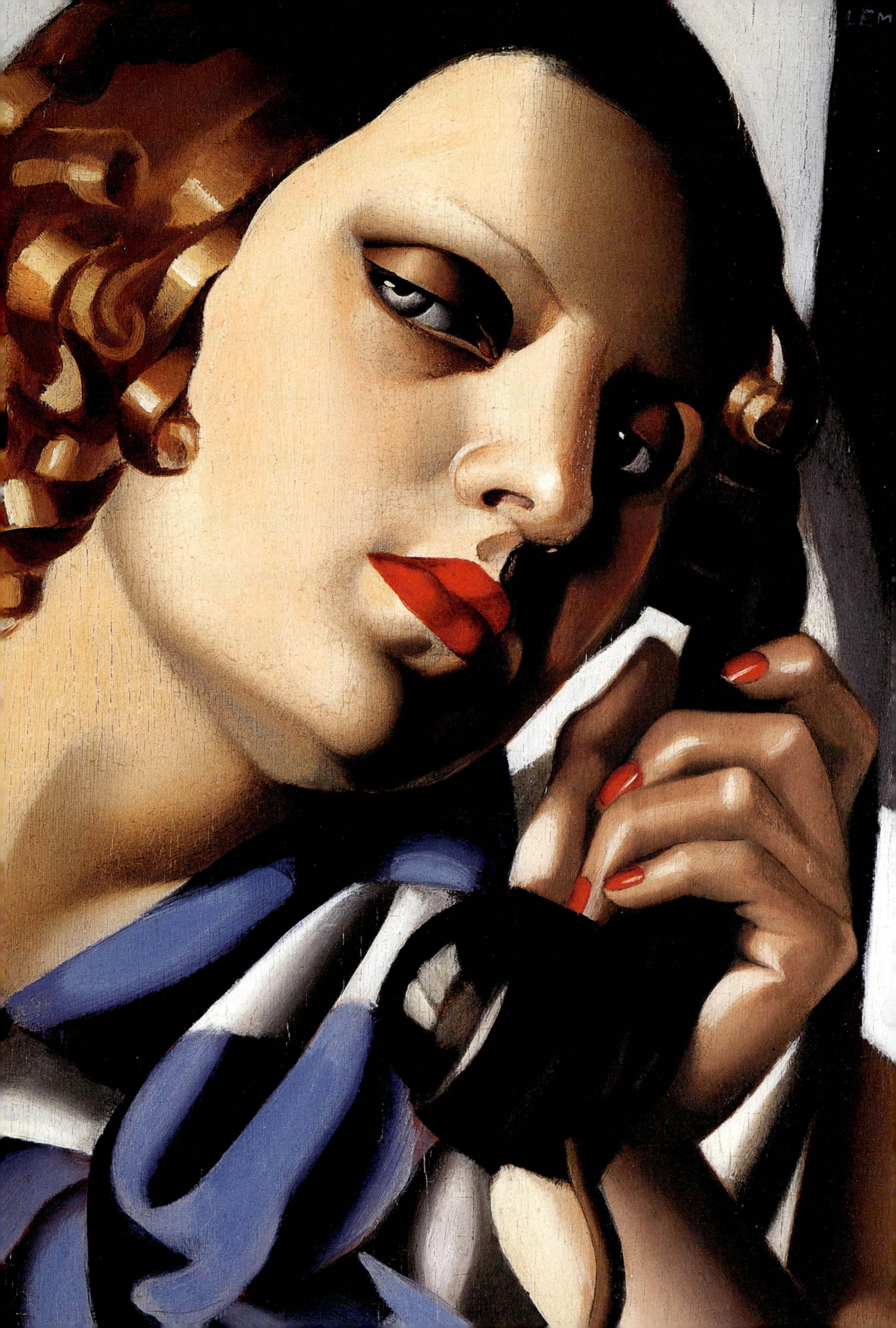

Tamara de Lempicka – Artist and *femme fatale*

Turn the clock back to the decade between 1919 and 1929. The conflict between the imperial powers that had triggered World War I was now over. It was the decade spanning the peace-making bid of the Treaty of Versailles and the Wall Street Crash that brought a seemingly indestructible economic system to its knees. These were turbulent times indeed – and this was the most fertile phase in the career of the Polish painter Tamara de Lempicka. Living in Paris, she showed a remarkable talent for capturing the mood of the moment, and her rise from impoverished young émigré to the toast of the Parisian art world was nothing short of meteoric. Never before had there been a decade of such upheaval, fuelled as it was by an inherent urge to transform all in its path while falling into step with the dynamic march of technical innovation and economic development.

The 1920s saw the emergence of a whole new world of engineering, technology, velocity and efficiency that was eagerly embraced. The pre-war revolution in art (Expressionism in Germany, Cubism in France, Futurism in Italy, Suprematism and Constructivism in Russia, as well as the continuing influence of Symbolism and Impressionism) was quickly followed by a radical attempt to restore order, echoed in the publication of Jean Cocteau's anthology of post-war essays *Le Rappel à l'ordre*, published in Paris in 1926. This call to order sought a return to mathematical and scientific objectivity as well as a reconsideration of certain rules in all the arts, from literature, music and painting to theatre and architecture. A return to the stylistic syntax of times past was meant to give artists the freedom to show – and apply – the inherent flaws and paradoxes of their predecessors. Artists were now expected to have 'style' rather than 'a style'.

One of the hallmarks of the 1920s lies in the rather odd phenomenon that it was not only the adherents of Surrealism but also the proponents of Realism and Neue Sachlichkeit (New Objectivity) who cast doubt upon the viability of realistic art. They questioned painting's capacity as a medium for the portrayal and imaging of reality. Consequently, the very concept of reality and the veracity of appearances were fundamentally called into question and, as such, became the focus of their work, spawning the quest for a differently constructed reality. Verism and Neue Sachlichkeit alike endeavoured to show up the countless flaws and contradictions of modern life, while Surrealism portrayed the inextricable link between the reality of dreams and the reality of the everyday as lying somewhere between the conscious and the subconscious.

What all the artists of this period – Expressionists, Dadaists and Cubists alike – had in common was their shared experience of war and their rejection of Impressionism. After the excesses of Expressionism, they now sought a greater visual sobriety devoid of all sentimentality. Whether or not Lempicka was actually aware of these contradictions in the artistic developments of the day, and whether or not she sought to convey them in her paintings, is a moot point. One thing, at least, is certain: she was actively involved in the discourse of the Paris art world and, in this respect, was typical of many of her contemporaries who adapted so easily at first to the pace of transition, using it to their advantage, only to stumble at the hurdle of unstoppable change.

The great counterpoints of the 1920s were Fernand Léger and Pablo Picasso. Picasso was the artist who rediscovered ancient mythology for his contemporaries, while Léger portrayed the myths of the technical age and its artefacts. In Léger's work, the focus is on man and machine in a kind of 'heroism of modern life'. Unlike the Neue Sachlichkeit view of humankind in which the individual despairs of his environment and the little man is at the mercy of a world he has created but cannot control, in this heroic view, the individual creates his own new

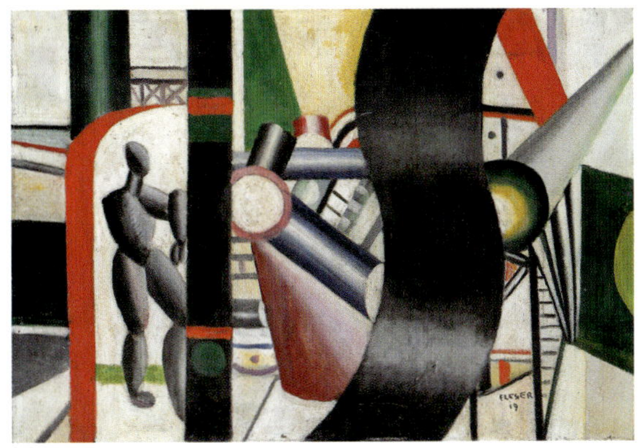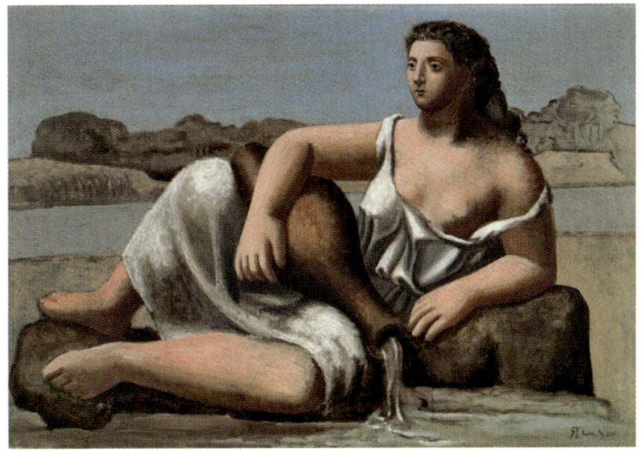

Fernand Léger, *Black Chauffeur*, 1919. Oil on canvas, 46 × 65 cm, private collection

Pablo Picasso, *The Source*, 1921. Oil on canvas, 64 × 90 cm, Moderna Museet, Stockholm

era and optimistically embraces modern developments. In contrast to, say, the Futurists, who unconditionally welcomed progress, Neue Sachlichkeit and Magical Realism artists turned against the continuously accelerating pace of life, against the new high-speed existence. The only alternative that artists seemed to have had, if they were to avoid descending into outmoded and lachrymose sentimentality, was to perfect a cool, objective view of everyday life. The same cool gaze with which objects had once been viewed was now turned to people as well and individuals were painted with the same detachment as things: "Seeking in the faces of people the distinctive characteristics of the era rather than the individuality of the person."[1] Lempicka swam with the tide of these new developments by choosing the style that suited her best: a cool, detached view of the very society of which she wanted so much to be a part.

Throughout her life, Tamara de Lempicka refused to make any serious statements about herself. This fact alone is indicative of her wish to construct a personality that may never actually have existed in this form. At the very least, it underlines her insistence that what we should consider and evaluate above all is her art, to which everything else should be secondary. The absence of any letters, diaries or other documents on which biographers normally base their descriptions of people's lives has been the bane of many an ambitious attempt to understand the personal history of Lempicka. One

sketch of the artist's life, to be approached with some caution
– though this is also part of its fascinating appeal – is by her
own daughter, Kizette. While Kizette's account does, to some
extent, attempt to lift the veil woven by her famous mother,[2]
her statements do at times – justifiably or not – take on the
resentful tone of the neglected and disappointed daughter.
Thanks to her intimate knowledge and her anecdotes, however, she provides insights that broaden and deepen our
understanding of one of the most important women artists of
the early twentieth century.

From Warsaw to Paris via St Petersburg   1898–1918

Tamara de Lempicka, née Gorska, was born in Warsaw in 1898
during the Russian occupation. Her parents belonged to the
wealthy aristocracy and coped remarkably well under the
circumstances by turning the situation to their financial
advantage. Indeed, their flexibility may even have laid the
foundations for Lempicka's own skill at adapting to her social
surroundings and drawing on any potentially advantageous
situation. It was a talent that was to stand
her in particularly good stead in
Paris. During the occupation,
many of Poland's leading
male intellectuals lived in
exile or emigration, leaving women to play a key
role in upholding and
nurturing Polish culture.
This explains why, in the
few anecdotes told by
Lempicka, it is always female
members of the family who played
an important role in her life.

Tamara aged thirteen, playing
Diabolo, Monte Carlo, 1911

Lempicka's first introduction to the world of art came at the
age of thirteen, when she accompanied her grandmother to

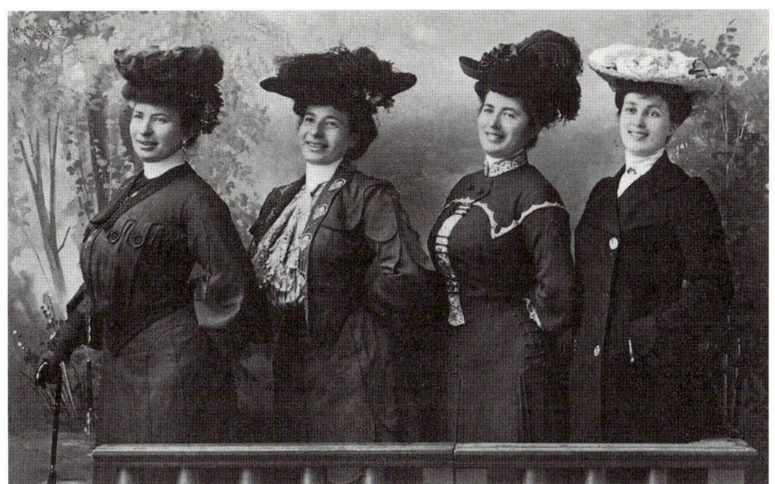

Italy and was taken to all the great museums of Florence, Rome and Venice. She returned to Warsaw in the spring of 1912, having undergone what was, to all intents and purposes, a crash-course in the history of Italian painting, especially the Renaissance. By the time World War I broke out, Lempicka was living in St Petersburg with her aunt. It had been her mother's decision to remarry that had prompted Lempicka, accustomed as she was to having her own way, to go and live instead with her wealthy Aunt Stefa and her husband.

In St Petersburg, Tamara was able to indulge for the first time in a life of real luxury. Her aunt and uncle had weekly dispatches of new clothes, fabrics, jewellery and furnishings sent to them from France. For the young teenager, such a lifestyle began to seem the only one worth aspiring to. Then, at one of her many visits to the opera, she met the rakish and attractive young lawyer Tadeusz Lempicki, who, according to her daughter Kizette, must have been "the most eligible bachelor in Petrograd" (St Petersburg having been renamed Petrograd in 1914). To the dismay of her family, who saw in him a womaniser and *bon vivant* unworthy of her attentions, Tamara conquered his heart. Tamara Gorska and Tadeusz Lempicki married in 1916 in Petrograd. It was an ostentatious ceremony and the bride's train stretched all the way from the altar to the church door.

Their happiness was short-lived. In 1917, Lenin declared a state of siege in Petrograd and, in the months that followed, the Cheka secret police spread chaos and terror, until the city's wealthy citizens feared not only for their possessions, but also for their lives. One night, Tadeusz was arrested without warning on suspicion of having links with the Tsarist secret police. His wife was unable to find out where he was or for how long he would be held. Lempicka's aunt and uncle had already fled to Copenhagen with their sons and begged their niece to follow them. But she did not want to leave the country without her husband. In an unprecedented act in which she secured rather more than just the sympathy and help of the Swedish consul, Lempicka succeeded in having her husband released from custody. She was allowed to travel to Finland and from there to Denmark, where she waited in the hope that her husband would soon follow. Tadeusz arrived in Copenhagen just six weeks later. But his imprisonment and his awareness of the price that his wife had probably paid for his freedom made him a changed man. The outgoing *bon vivant* became sullen, introspective and dissatisfied. Lempicka did not put up with this for long and, while still in Copenhagen, embarked on an affair with a diplomat. It marked the beginning of what was probably a long and acrimonious struggle between the young couple.

Lempicka and Tadeusz followed the former's family to Paris, where things rapidly went from bad to worse. Lempicka soon realised that, in the circles in which she moved in Paris, the easiest way to become rich and famous was to put on a sophisticated and worldly air by shrouding herself in mystery and rubbing shoulders with artists and *bohémiens*. Tadeusz, on the other hand, felt quite out of place.

Why Paris? In the early years of the twentieth century, Vienna had been the undisputed cultural capital of Europe. From around 1910 until the mid-1920s, the focus shifted to Berlin, which became a melting pot for a motley crew. Berlin was the very embodiment of Fritz Lang's *Metropolis* – an explosive mix

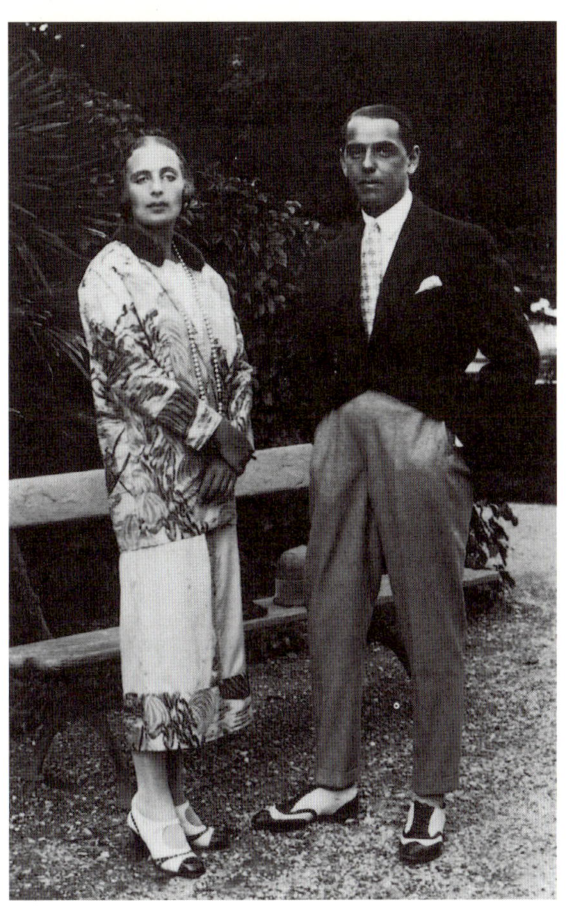

The artist with her first
husband, Tadeusz de
Lempicki, Paris, 1920

of social strata from the proletariat to the bourgeoisie and the aristocracy. Paris was different. In the course of the previous decades, it had maintained an urban continuity that did not reflect the epochal mood of change prevailing elsewhere. The photographs by that great chronicler of Paris, Eugène Atget, show the same 'capital of the nineteenth century' (as Walter Benjamin described it) that still survived in the 1920s. "The city had remained an agglomeration of different quarters, a huddle of large villages, each with its own characteristics, a vital, hospitable, pulsating organism with its arteries, its entrails, its juices, its nooks and crannies, and with thousands of people, from the heroic to the stranded, flurrying around inside it."[3]

The Great Depression of 1929 put an end to the cosy sense of security, even in Paris. The political and economic developments of the 1930s made their mark on the centres of the European avant-garde, gradually shifting the focus from Vienna, Berlin and Paris to the other side of the Atlantic. Nevertheless, in the early 1920s, Paris was still a magnet for all manner of émigrés, especially for the artists and bohemians who frequented the cafés of Montparnasse. Because the Gorskis and Lempickis spoke fluent French, there was at least no language barrier. The presence of other Polish and Russian émigrés also gave them reason for optimism; by the time the Lempickis came to Paris, almost a quarter of a million Russian and Polish citizens had settled there.

The Path to Success   1919–1924

Lempicka is unlikely to have been entirely penniless when she arrived in Paris. However, in spite of the support of her family, she soon found herself in financial straits and became acutely aware of the need to find a lucrative source of income to support her little family. Her daughter Kizette was born around 1920 – the exact date is unknown and not even Kizette has provided any precise information on this. Her husband, who was unable or perhaps unwilling to find work for a long time, could not be relied on as a breadwinner. He hardly ever left the hotel room, nagged at her constantly and spent his time reading detective novels. Lempicka, on the other hand, had learned at an early age to stand on her own two feet, and she did so in her new surroundings.

Lempicka's sister Adrienne, who had moved to Paris before her with their mother, had been studying architecture at the École des Beaux-Arts since the beginning of the 1920s. She was the one who inspired Lempicka's wish to become a painter. One of Lempicka's favourite anecdotes was of a momentous conversation with her sister at a party given by their Aunt Stefa towards the end of 1919. Adrienne had taken her aside because she had noticed her sister seemed somewhat out of sorts. On being asked what was the matter, Lempicka had replied: "We have no money … and he beats me." "Then you must work." … "I said, 'Work? Work what? All the grand duchesses, they were Chanel mannequins … but they had slim figures.'"[4]

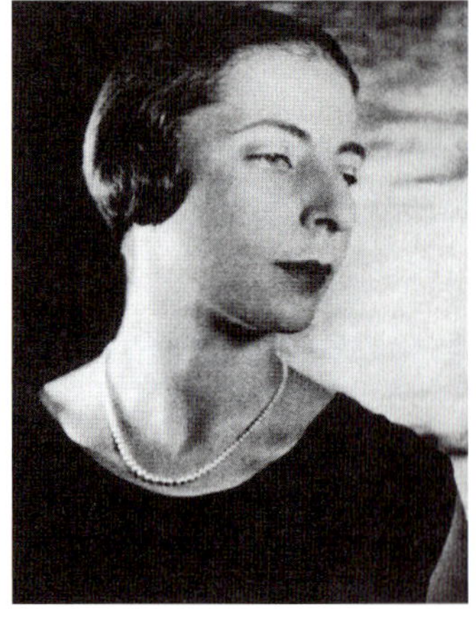

Adrienne Gurwick-Gorska, the artist's sister, *c.* 1920

Adrienne then reminded Lempicka of her talent for painting and suggested that she take classes at the Académie de la Grande Chaumière and sell her paintings to support her family. After giving it some thought, Lempicka willingly accepted the idea. It was the only way she could see of escaping her marital problems and her financial difficulties. Lempicka set about her plan with energy and persistence, determined to become rich and famous within the shortest possible time,

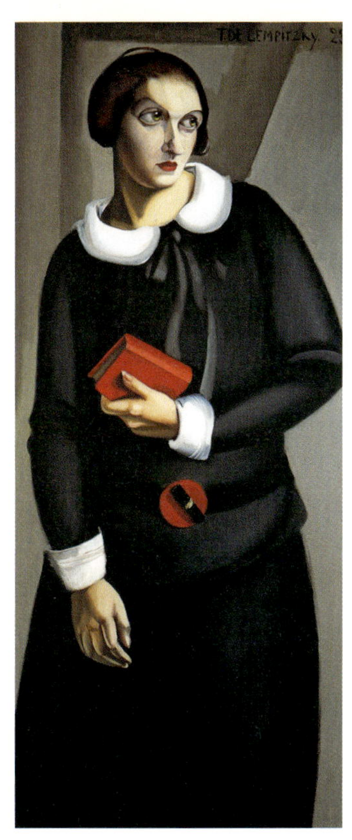

Woman in a Black Dress, 1923. Oil on canvas, 195 × 60.5 cm, Wolfgang Joop Collection, Hamburg

just as she had planned to do as a teenager in Petrograd. She attended classes at the Académie during the morning, afternoon and evening sessions. In the early morning she would go to the market and between classes she even found time to cook for Tadeusz, who showed nothing like his wife's resourcefulness. She would often spend her evenings in the cafés of Montparnasse (especially in the famous Deux Magots), which had replaced the salons of the nineteenth century as hubs of communication, discussing painting, politics and life in general with the artists of Paris. The only time she had left to paint her first still lifes and, later, some portraits, was at night when she was not arguing with her husband. Just three years after that conversation with Adrienne, Tamara de Lempicka was able to exhibit her works at the Salon d'Automne.

The artist remained as secretive about her training as she would about every other personal detail of her life. It is not certain whether, as she claimed, she had studied at the Academy in St Petersburg – a claim she retracted towards the end of her life. In Paris, she is known to have studied at the Académie de la Grande Chaumière and to have received instruction from Maurice Denis and André Lhote, whose ability she later, in typical style, disparaged. She systematically played down the influence of her teachers in order to present herself as an independent artist. "For a few weeks I attended the classes of Maurice Denis and then the Academy of André Lhote. But I had no interest in the tuition. I couldn't help being bored … This is why I stayed only a few months with André Lhote."[5]

In some of her works, however, the influence of Lhote cannot be overlooked; in formal terms, at least, Lempicka did learn quite a lot from him. His theories gave her the tools with which to adapt Cubist innovations for her own painting. She learned to balance compositional elements and handle space with particular sensitivity. Above all, her use of only a few clearly defined colours became the hallmark of her oeuvre. Lhote taught her to use only two or three colours in a picture and to use grey as a binding element between fields of colour. His influence as her mentor even went so far that he was able to imbue in Lempicka his own enthusiasm for Ingres. Lhote himself took little interest in the avant-garde, in spite of the fact that Paris at the time was a hotbed of the Dada movement, with such figures as Tzara, Céline, Picabia, Breton and others discussing their ideas in cafés, organising attention-grabbing events and generally shaping the entire cultural climate of the city. Not even the Surrealists, whose movement was becoming increasingly influential, were able to sway Lempicka. She viewed the potent symbolism of their pictures with scepticism. As for Marinetti and the Futurists who also propagated their revolutionary ideas in Paris, all that we know of her involvement with them is through one of her many anecdotes. One afternoon, in a Paris café, Marinetti, author of the Futurist Manifesto, was expounding on one of his revolutionary ideas about destroying the past, and talked himself into such a frenzy that he incited his audience and followers to "Burn down the Louvre!" The eager group then allegedly poured out onto the street, hell-bent on driving to the Louvre in Lempicka's little car. Unfortunately, however, she had parked illegally and her car had been towed away. On the way to the police station, the crowd dwindled – as did their enthusiasm for burning down the Louvre. Marinetti at least had the decency to accompany her to the police station. Lempicka may have been aware of the various avant-garde movements of the day, but, as this anecdote illustrates, she tended to look at them with the eyes of a detached observer, rather than becoming involved herself.

Though she would later deny the influence of her teachers, Lempicka took her early art studies very seriously. She would visit the Louvre every day, copying the heads and hands of the Renaissance masters, studying the handling of light in Netherlandish paintings and the way the Italians used colour. Even the towering figures of modern art that she would later denigrate, most notably Picasso, were carefully observed. It was, however, first and foremost the French Cubists who left their traces in her paintings – for instance, she adapted the Manhattan skyline developed by Alber Gleizes after his visit to New York as a frequent background element in her portraits. Portraiture seemed the perfect vehicle for her determined ambition to make money quickly and gain a foothold in Parisian society. One anecdote she liked to relate in this respect tells how she decided to buy herself a bracelet every time she had sold two paintings, until the diamonds and jewels reached from her wrist to her elbow – a target she achieved far sooner than she imagined. With her astonishing talent for channelling the trends of the 1920s in a direction of her own, giving her portraits their distinctively aloof, objective and yet emotionally charged air, the young émigré soon achieved what she had set out to do and quickly became the brightest star in the Paris art firmament.

Lempicka's images oscillate between smouldering sensuality and cool classicism, adding a whole new dimension to the history of painting in the 1920s and 1930s. Nowhere are the aspects of Neue Sachlichkeit interpreted with such sensuality and eroticism as in her figures. She became the *femme fatale* of her day, a diva at the very centre of society and a painter whose portraits mirrored her social surroundings. Around 1922, when she was beginning to have a taste of artistic and social success, Lempicka juggled the life of a student, painter, wife, mother, breadwinner and seductress. She smoked three packets of cigarettes a day, took a daily dose of valerian (and any amount of cocaine at various jazz club parties) and was confident that she would soon have *le tout Paris* at her feet as the perfect embodiment of the 'modern woman'.

Success also brought with it a strangely arrogant attitude to the artistic trends of modern painting: "At the beginning of my career, I was looking around me and could see only complete destruction in painting. I was disgusted with the banality into which art had fallen. I felt Picasso embodied the novelty of destruction. I revolted; I looked for a *métier* that did not exist any longer. I was working very fast and with an easy brush. I aimed at technique, *métier*, simplicity, and good taste. My goal: do not copy. Create a new style, colours light and bright, return to elegance in my models … Cézanne would draw a few apples, but the apples were badly drawn. And the colours – why is it all so dirty? … The Impressionists painted from imagination more than from nature; they did not paint well; they did not care about technique. I said to myself: they are dirty. It's not precise. Mind the precision. A painting has to be neat and clean. I was the first woman who did clear painting – and that was the success of my painting. Among a hundred paintings, you could recognise mine. And the galleries began to put me in the best rooms, always in the centre, because my painting attracted people. It was neat; it was finished."

By the mid-1920s, she was beginning to attract widespread attention. Her Salon exhibitions brought ever more sales and new commissions. In 1925, the Ministère des Beaux-Arts, the Association des Arts Décorateurs and the Ville de Paris inaugurated the first Art Déco exhibition. This exhibition in 1925 marked the zenith of the decorative arts, especially French. Superbly crafted one-off pieces, from earrings to complete interiors, were celebrated here in an ostentatious display of luxury. The term Art Moderne, which had recently come into vogue, came to express an exquisite yet anachronistic quest for style in a vain attempt to unite the disparate developments of the decade in a blend of geometric formulae, conventionally stylised Art Nouveau elements and recently discovered East Asian folk art that pandered to a taste for opulence.

The exhibition included the work of leading couturiers, a pavilion by one of France's most famous architects, Mallet-Stevens, and paintings by Robert Delaunay, Fernand Léger, Le Corbusier and Pierre Jeanneret. Other now world-famous participants included Raoul Dufy, René Lalique, Cartier, Erté and Pierre Chareau. Le Corbusier, however, is said to have railed vehemently against the spirit of the exhibition, calling it "a state-sanctioned waste of money" and claiming that the exhibits were, without exception, trivia that he disdained "in the name of all and in the name of reason, moral and good taste."

Although the exhibition did not actually include any paintings by Lempicka, the Polish artist seems to have been in the right place at the right time in order to profit from the reactions triggered by the Expo. She proved to be the very epitome of the Art Déco artist, tapping directly into the spirit of the age. By concentrating entirely on a single genre, portraiture, she avoided the trap of the merely decorative and superficially pleasing that was to be the downfall of so many of her contemporaries. She painted the wealthy and the aristocratic, as well as her own friends and acquaintances (not to mention her many lovers) – people who were gradually losing their public status and could no longer be certain of retaining their positions of power and influence. Most of them withdrew into a private life that revolved around parties, leisure and superficial pleasure. They channelled their energies into their outward appearance, their clothing, demeanour and style – the very things that would lend themselves to the cool, detached portraiture of Tamara de Lempicka.

After World War I, members of almost every social stratum found the very basis of their existence in crisis. The world was out of joint. A desire to hold fast to the clarity of the quotidian and the undeniable reality of the visible was triggered by a yearning for security and by the pressing need to find a new direction and a new sense of identity in a world ravaged by war. This need was also felt by Lempicka's socialite sitters as they watched their sphere of influence diminishing. It was around this time that a new Realism emerged in most of Europe, as in the USA, and soon began to play an important role. In France, Picasso developed a pluralism of style with clearly realistic tendencies. In Italy, the avant-garde periodicals 'Valori Plastici' and 'Novecento' were launched. In Germany, the gallery owner G.F. Hartlaub was exhibiting Neue Sachlichkeit, Verism and Neo-Classicism. In America, the terms 'Precionist View' and 'American Scene' were coined to describe a new generation of painters. Everywhere, the technical possibilities of photography were embraced, as was its supposedly objective view that could capture all the phenomena of the world without distinction or prejudice, unemotionally and unsentimentally. "This view shaped by scepticism and disillusionment distrusted all visions. It focused on the banality and everyday things of the city and its environment, on seemingly unprepossessing subjects. It had no fear whatsoever of 'ugliness'. ... There is no involvement or commitment in the cool gaze. It isolates things the way it isolates people."[6]

But the underlying mood of the time was not only restorative; it was shaped by an attempt to form a new reality out of the shards and debris of the reality that had been shattered. In this, it differed from earlier forms of realism. Now it was more a case of finding a firm foothold again after the chaos of war (Jean Cocteau's *Le rappel à l'ordre* being a case in point).

Italy: Passions and Patrons 1925–1926

Lempicka organised her work as an artist, from her training to her exhibitions and even the sale of her paintings, entirely single-handedly. She took on the role of producer, manager, advertising executive and salesperson – only Colette Weil, at whose gallery she exhibited in 1930 and 1931, acted temporarily as a dealer for her. In 1925, for instance, Lempicka visited Italy again, this time with her mother and her daughter, mainly to study the works of art in Rome and Florence. On the return journey, she stopped in Milan to visit the famous gallery owner Duke Emmanuele Castelbarco. She showed him some photographs of her paintings and actually managed to persuade him to mount an exhibition of more than thirty of her works in his 'Bottega di Poesia'. Having agreed that the exhibition should open in November of the same year, Lempicka immediately set to work the moment she returned to

Paris in order to be able to send that amount of work to Italy within the prescribed time. Her boundless energy and her determination to achieve what she had set out to do helped her to complete this Herculean task within only a few months. Castelbarco also introduced her to some of the most important figures in Italian society, which in turn led to some of her finest portraits, such as that of the Marquis Guido Sommi Picenardi, the husband of Princess Pignatelli.

The artist's own aim of "painting as many paintings as quickly as possible and turning them into money quickly" could only be achieved if she worked within the boundaries of social norms with calculated provocation. Her quest for recognition also led her to seek the acquaintance of socially influential persons. It is particularly interesting to note that she tried to win the patronage of the poet and politician Gabriele d'Annunzio by making quite unambiguous advances towards him, in spite of the fact that he was almost forty years her senior. Born in 1863, d'Annunzio had studied in Rome and Naples before meeting the actress Eleonora Duse, to whom he had dedicated a number of his plays and with whom he had embarked on the first of many affairs. Politically involved, he became a member of parliament for the extreme right in 1898–1900 and soon counted among Mussolini's friends. His love of luxury left him deeply in debt and, in 1908, he emigrated to France, returning to Italy only in 1915. He was ardently in favour of Italy entering the war, was wounded as an air force officer and led an 'expeditionary force' to capture the port of Fiume in 1919/20. Since then he has been revered as a national hero. D'Annunzio died at Gardone Riviera in 1938.

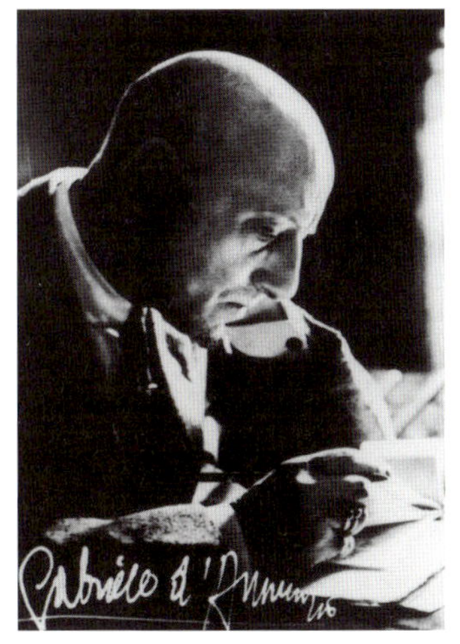

Gabriele d'Annunzio at his desk, *c.* 1925

"In the clutches of her hunger, having barely tasted of success and salivating for celebrity in her own right as an artist, she could hardly avoid wishing to paint the man whose personality had marked an epoch and whom everyone she knew admired and praised. A Lempicka portrait of d'Annunzio would be something to see, a masterpiece well beyond anything … At this point, she was more successful socially than artistically and she knew it. But if others did not take her painting as seriously as she did, that was their problem – not hers. D'Annunzio seemed infatuated with her, and that flattered her. With her 'killer instinct' she thought she could both enjoy his attention and use it in the service of her art," wrote her daughter, Kizette.[7]

A letter written by Lempicka in 1926 to d'Annunzio says that she wants to confide in him because she believes that only he can believe her and not think her mad. "Perhaps one day, one evening, one night, you'll feel an irresistible urge to speak to me – and then you'll write me again. I wait. I hope. I want."

D'Annunzio, who had, of course, heard of the beautiful and extravagant artist, wanted the same and so he invited her to spend a week at his house near Lake Garda. Lempicka's husband Tadeusz watched the situation unfolding from afar and sent his wife a telegram every other day demanding her return. He knew or suspected that she only ever painted portraits of her lovers (or that at least she was in love with her sitters). D'Annunzio's villa was already full of potential and existing lovers – a young ballerina, an aging pianist, and the housekeeper. It was not unlike a brothel. The arrival of the 'beautiful Pole' was regarded with some displeasure, but her stay there was to be even more complicated than expected. In spite of her ardent desire to paint the poet's portrait, Lempicka was reluctant to accept his advances. She held back, repeatedly insisting on her real reason for being there, until he eventually lost his patience with her and (as he claimed) more or less showed her the door. Lempicka neither painted his portrait nor had an affair with him – these two strong characters seemed to have little in common and, according to Lempicka, her early departure came as a relief to both of them. Aelis Mazoyer, d'Annunzio's lover and housekeeper, recorded some sordid little details of this tragicomedy in her diary, which was published in 1977, much to the annoyance of Lempicka, who refused point-blank to be associated in any way with "the vulgar tittle-tattle of some servant."

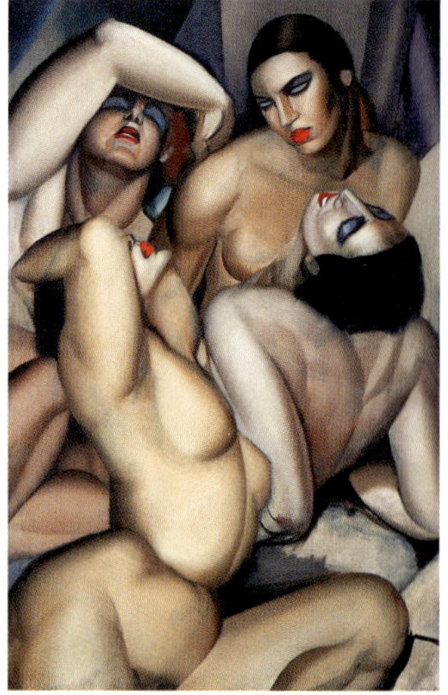

Group of Four Female Nudes,
1925. Oil on canvas,
130 × 81 cm,
private collection

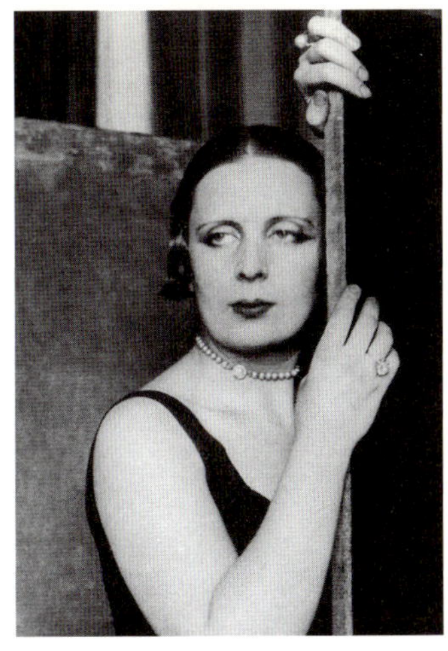

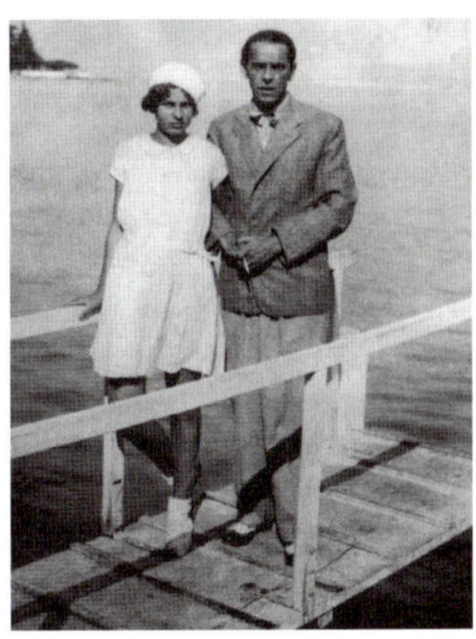

Tamara de Lempicka behind
a screen, *c.* 1927

Tadeusz and Kizette at Lake
Como, *c.* 1927/28

Paris: Life in the Limelight   1927–1939

Soon, Tamara de Lempicka no longer had any need for such patrons as Gabriele d'Annunzio. The young Polish émigré was a household name and the most sought-after portraitist in Europe. She could command as much as 2,000 dollars for a portrait that often took her less than three weeks to finish.

Her financial problems were a thing of the past and she spent her money on the flamboyant clothes and hats that turned heads in the nightclubs, shops and restaurants she frequented. Art and fashion critics wrote about her, about her paintings, her hats, her style, her daughter and her family life.

She seemed at last to have reached her goal. The Lempickis no longer lived in a shabby hotel room, but in a fine house with a garden on the rue Martin. But none of this could prevent the end of her marriage to Tadeusz, who accused her of neglecting her family for the sake of her career.

On a business trip to Warsaw in 1927, he met Irene Spiess, daughter of a wealthy industrialist who owned one of Poland's biggest pharmaceutical companies. It was 'love at first sight'. Tadeusz finally left Lempicka who, needless to say, could not accept such humiliating rejection with good grace. As their daughter Kizette so shrewdly summed up: "De Lempicki may not have been the kind of man she needed, but he was her husband, her retainer, part of her court. When he ran away – for another woman – that left a gap in her existence, like a gnawing in her stomach she could not ignore."[8]

Lempicka travelled to Poland to meet him and both tried, unsuccessfully, to patch up their relationship on a trip to Monte Carlo. But all they achieved was painful bickering and accusations: "Who do you think you're talking to? I'm an artist! You're a nobody who's too dumb even to have an affair with a pretty girl instead of the first mouse who runs across your path."[9] They divorced in 1928.

That same year, Tamara de Lempicka met her long-time patron, the Hungarian Baron Raoul Kuffner, personally for the first time. One day, he visited her studio to ask her to paint a portrait of his mistress, the famous Andalusian dancer Nana de Herrera. When the painting was finished – and having made some very direct comments about the woman whose taste in clothes she regarded as incredibly bad – Lempicka herself became the baron's lover. By now, she was able to afford a huge apartment and studio in rue Méchain on the Left Bank, and commissioned the Art Déco architect and designer Roger Mallet-Stevens to furnish and decorate it. Every detail of the apartment was discussed and designed around the œuvre of Tamara de Lempicka. Even the upholstery had her initials woven into it. "Yes, it would provide just the right backdrop, stark and sleek. Here she would throw the grand parties she had always dreamed of. Here she was sure she would talk to the best minds of her generation, sleep with the most stunning women and the most handsome men in Europe, paint the greatest paintings Paris had ever seen."[10] An Italian journalist described one of the many parties that the artist gave at her beautiful apartment: "The painter received the crème de la crème of Paris … In 1937, for instance, she received the Ambassadors of Greece and Peru, van Dongen and Princess Gargarin, Kisling and Dr Woronow, the Duchess of Villarosa and Lady Chamberlain, her teacher

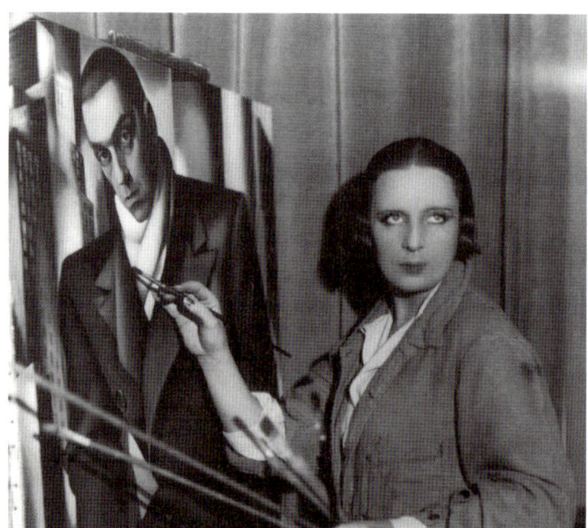

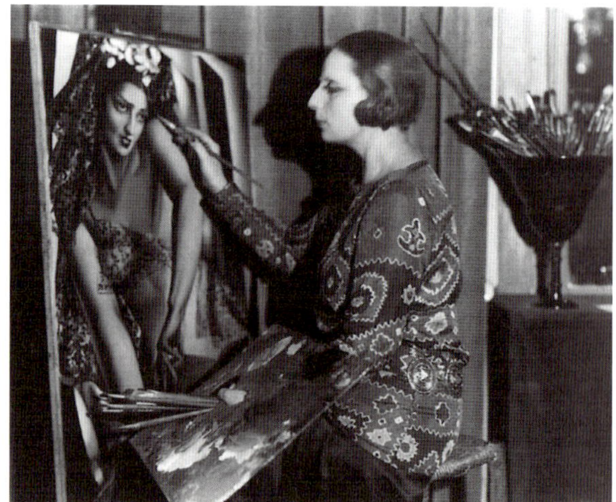

Lempicka in front of the portrait of her husband, Tadeusz, *c.* 1928

Lempicka in front of her portrait of Nana de Herrera, *c.* 1927

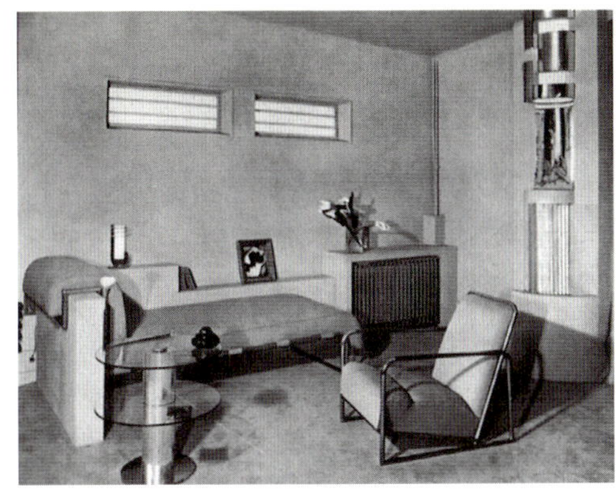
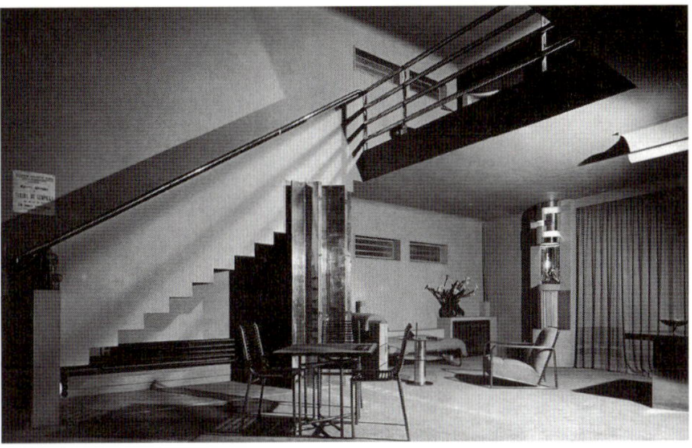

André Lhote and the Clemenceaus. The beauty, elegance and reputation of the artist were at the centre of a fluctuating circle of friends and acquaintances; the people around her were like planets, large and small, bright and wan. Many reporters went into sheer ecstasy at the very sight of her … thrilled by her hands, her hair, her clothes … One journalist … was breathless at the sight of this 'tall and slender something' with the 'magnificent shock of golden-red hair that fell to her shoulders." All the world is awestruck and can express this only by exaggeration."[11]

1928/29 marks a turning point in the personal life and career of Tamara de Lempicka. Having finally separated from her husband in 1928, she now began asserting herself as an artist in France (the Museum in Nantes, for instance, purchased her 1926 *Portrait of Kizette in Pink*) and French art critics began to take her seriously.

In September 1929, Lempicka left Paris and boarded a luxury liner for the USA to paint the portrait of a young millionaire's fiancée. Her extortionate fee was accepted without question. Having planned to stay for three weeks, she was still there several months later. Kizette had to spend Christmas alone with her grandmother, who was so infuriated by her daughter's behaviour that she threw all Tamara's hats on the fire. Lempicka had her hands full preparing an exhibition at the Carnegie Institute in Pittsburgh and taking on new commissions. In the end, she spent Christmas with a wealthy and attractive man, whose name she never divulged, at his ranch in New Mexico. There was no question by now of her being able to spend Christmas at home with her family.

When she did eventually return to Europe, times were beginning to change. The world was sliding into economic crisis and the success of recent years could not be sustained. In America, everyone had been eager to profit from the boom that had followed World War I. As private consumption increased, stock prices mirrored the strong dollar exchange rate, attracting private investors hoping to make their fortune. In the final phase of the economic boom, marked by yet another increase in the dollar exchange rate, many ordinary people were taking out loans to buy shares. The rate of growth was so rapid that it seemed remarkably easy to pay back the loans and the interest within a very short time and still make a profit. Nobody expected the bubble to burst, let alone a long-term crisis. On 23 October 1929, however, there was a run on the stock exchange. It continued the following day. Panic began to set in. Many people were now selling their shares to save what they could. On the afternoon of 28 October, there was another rush to sell. This time, the banks could do little to stem the flow. But it was only the beginning of a long and deep economic depression: by 1932, share prices had fallen to more than 80 per cent below their previous high. The entire American banking system crashed. Industrial production went into recession and the number of unemployed soared from 1.5 million in 1929 to almost 13 million in 1933 – one quarter of the entire labour force.

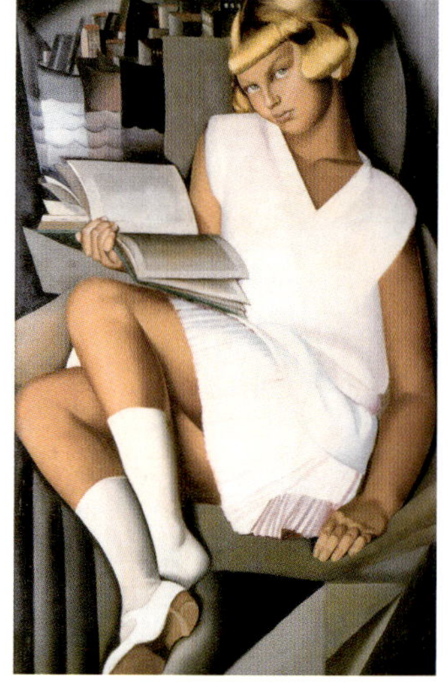

Kizette in Pink, c. 1926.
Oil on canvas, 116 × 73 cm,
Musée des Beaux-Arts de
Nantes, Nantes

The American crisis drew Europe into its vortex. France and Germany, which had run up high debts in the wake of the war, were particularly badly affected. As the financial crisis took hold in America, loan repayments were suddenly being demanded. Many companies were simply not in a position to pay. The banks that had brokered the loans between the American lenders and the European creditors in the first place came under pressure themselves. The situation was further exacerbated by an outbreak of panic, especially in Germany, where many still remembered the rampant inflation that had followed the end of World War I, and began withdrawing their money from bank accounts to invest in what they saw as more secure commodities. The crisis also triggered a fall in industrial production in Germany, where unemployment rose to more than six million. This was the fertile soil on which the fatal seed of National Socialism fell.

At first, the successful Polish émigré, who at last seemed to have achieved all she aimed for, did not want to accept what was happening. Similarly, the eternally youthful Lempicka would not accept that she could not avoid the process of aging. One revealing anecdote that she particularly liked to tell was how, on the advice of a good friend, she had once taken a break from her social commitments and the art world in order to recuperate from a nervous stomach disorder. She had applied to attend a convent-run boarding school for girls in Florence and had been accepted. She had then changed her hair and make-up to fit the role and had enjoyed spending her free afternoons flirting with Florentine adolescents until her art teacher finally blew her cover (having allegedly recognised her). Lempicka frequently told this story (or was it a fairy story?) with evident delight to prove that even at the age of thirty-five she had been able to pass as a teenager.

In 1933, Baroness Kuffner died on her Hungarian country estate, and her bereaved husband lost no time in asking Lempicka for her hand in marriage. After some hesitation, she accepted his proposal. Although she did not love him, he was able to offer her many of the things she had always wanted – wealth and, more importantly still, a title. She was now Baroness Kuffner. He allayed her doubts by assuring her that he had no intention of interfering in her life and that she would be able to live and work as before. When the National Socialists took power in Germany, even Lempicka could no longer ignore the situation and began urging her husband to sell up and go to America with her. Her experience of the Russian Revolution some twenty years before had sensitised her to certain developments and brought back unpleasant memories. She did not want to lose her possessions once again.

Looking for a New Beginning 1939–1980

But the political situation was not the only reason why Lempicka was so eager to make a new start. Her artistic career was stagnating, as was Art Déco itself. She was falling out of fashion and her portraits no longer seemed to be at the cutting edge. Although the artist continued to appear, flamboyantly dressed, at parties, nightclubs and dinner parties, she increasingly came to be seen more as an eccentric figure than as the fêted artist of the twenties. The Kuffners spent more and more of their time travelling in Italy and Switzerland. In 1939, shortly before the outbreak of war, the Baron finally listened to his wife, sold most of his estate and declared himself willing to accompany her to America.

The Kuffners moved to Beverly Hills, the ideal place for a life of empty gestures and superficial beauty. They soon gained a foothold in society, throwing parties just as they had done in Europe and trying to ignore the political situation. It was not long before the Hollywood greats were knocking at their door: Charles Boyer, Walter Pidgeon, Conchita Pignatelli, Lorna Hearst, Vicky Baum and even Greta Garbo. In 1939, Lempicka opened a one-woman exhibition at the Paul Reinhart gallery, followed by further exhibitions at Julian Levy in New York, at the Milwaukee Institute of Art and elsewhere. But her energy, creativity and her talent for capturing the spirit of the time seemed to have abandoned her in America. The media responded accordingly, describing her as 'the painting baroness', reducing her to a mere figure of interest whose works were not taken particularly seriously and did not sell well. In 1942, the Kuffners moved to New York.

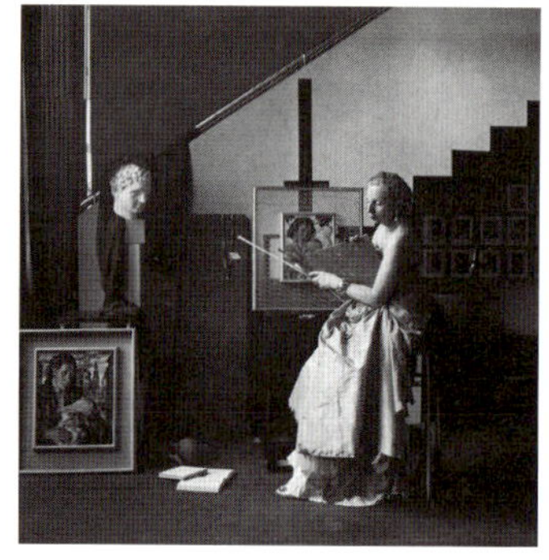

The artist in her studio in rue Méchain, Paris, *c.* 1937

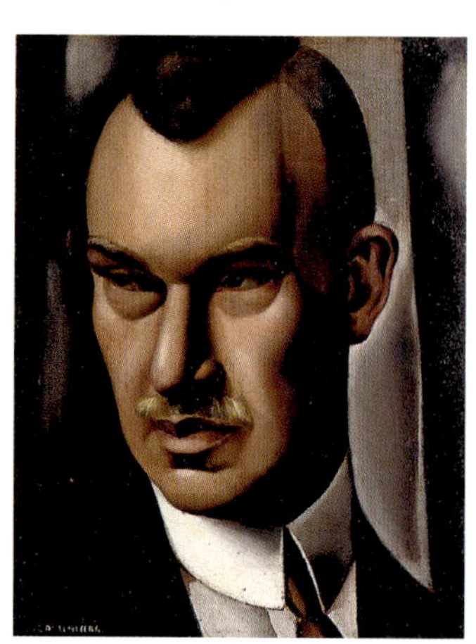

Portrait of a Man (Baron Kuffner), 1928. Oil on wood, 35 × 27 cm, Musée national d'art moderne, Paris

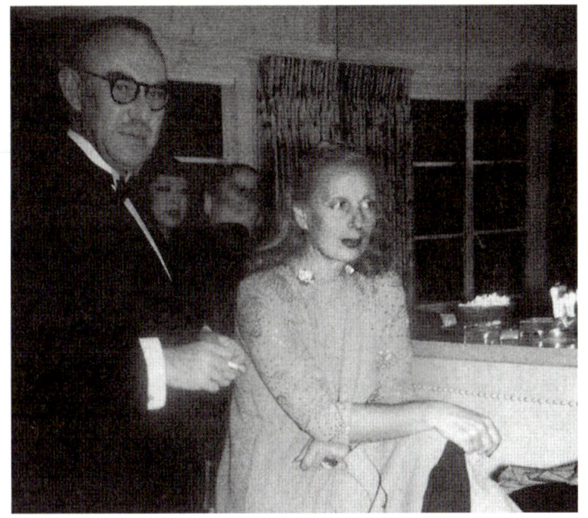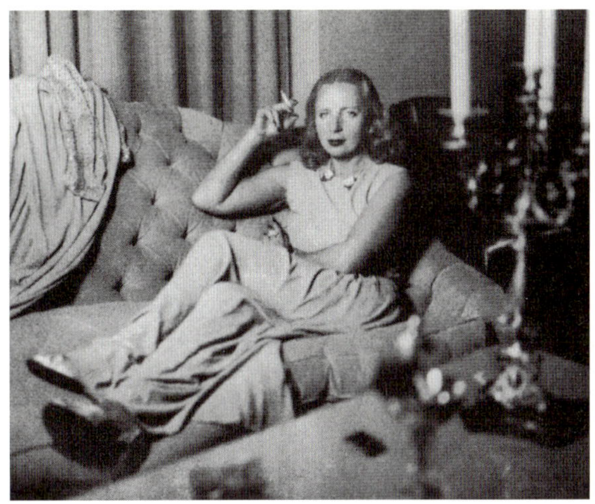

Raoul and Tamara Kuffner on a cruise, 1938

Lempicka in her Hollywood residence, *c.* 1940

In America, artistic development called for something that Lempicka may not have been able to provide. Paris had lost its status as the hub of the art world and, with the immigration of many European intellectuals and artists, New York had now taken its place. European scientists, philosophers, artists, poets, architects, film makers and musicians had an enormous influence on American intellectual life and made a crucial contribution to the emergence of a home-grown avant-garde. The 1913 Armory Show, which included European works by Symbolists, Post-Impressionists, Fauves and Cubists, had kick-started the American art scene, which had increasingly emancipated itself from the European influence. In New York, the émigrés felt that anything was possible. Their ideas became more radical, more independent, more grandiose. William van Alen's Chrysler Building (1928–30), for instance – pure Art Déco – could not have been built in such monumental form in Europe.

It was perhaps this atmosphere of change that made it impossible for an artist like Tamara de Lempicka to adapt and find a place amid the euphoria of the new. Perhaps it was the loss of the Old Paris that prevented her from starting afresh on the other side of the Atlantic. In the America of the 1940s, she found that the social circles in which she had moved so easily in Paris and which she had so perfectly mirrored in her

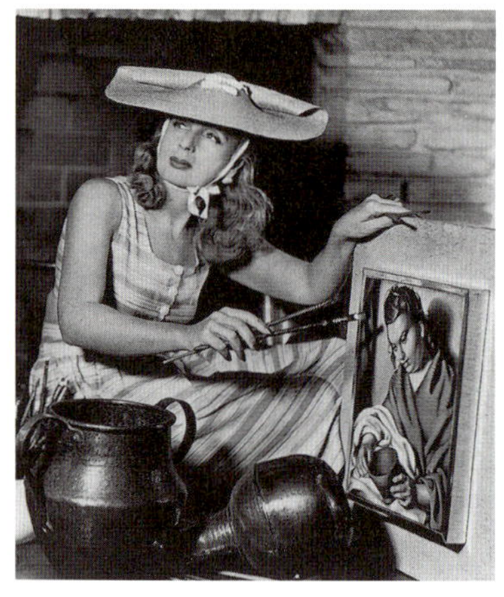

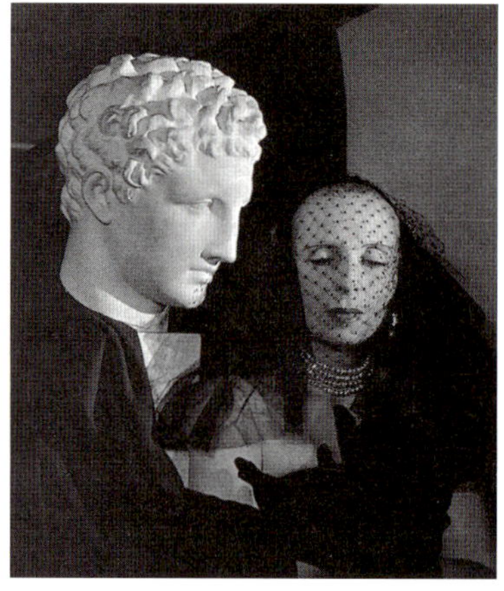

Lempicka in her Beverly Hills residence, 1941

Willy Maywald, Lempicka with classical bust, 1949. © Assoc. Willy Maywald – ADAGP

portraits, had lost all their influence. Indeed, in the eyes of the younger generation, it was that very society that was to be held responsible for the catastrophic events of the previous decade. Almost overnight, Tamara de Lempicka had fallen out of favour. It is not hard to imagine how this parade of the wealthy and the beautiful, dukes and princes, with their jewels and furs and pathos-laden poses, must have looked to the new generation of the 1950s.

Lempicka once again concentrated all her energy on her art. She developed a new style, first of all by changing her subject matter and no longer painting portraits only of wealthy and beautiful people, but of an old man with a guitar, the mother superior with a tear rolling down her cheek, and refugees with little children. But none of these paintings radiated the artist's former power. They were almost unbearably saccharine and melodramatic. Patrons and art lovers did not thank her for the change and soon turned their backs on Lempicka. A 1955 exhibition of these paintings at André Weil in Paris went almost unnoticed.

In the 1960s, the artist made one last attempt, working this time on abstract paintings using a palette knife. After some unambiguous reviews and unsuccessful exhibitions, she decided never to exhibit again and retired completely to her ivory tower. In 1962, her husband, Baron Kuffner, died.

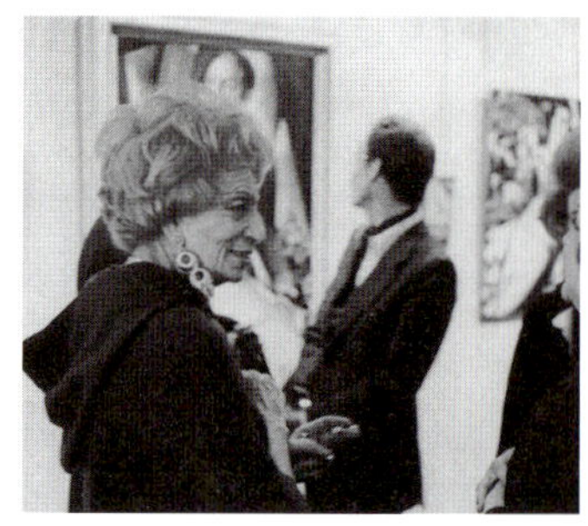

Lempicka at the opening of her retrospective exhibition at the Galerie du Luxembourg, 1972

Lempicka with her grand-daughters Chacha and Victoria, 1963

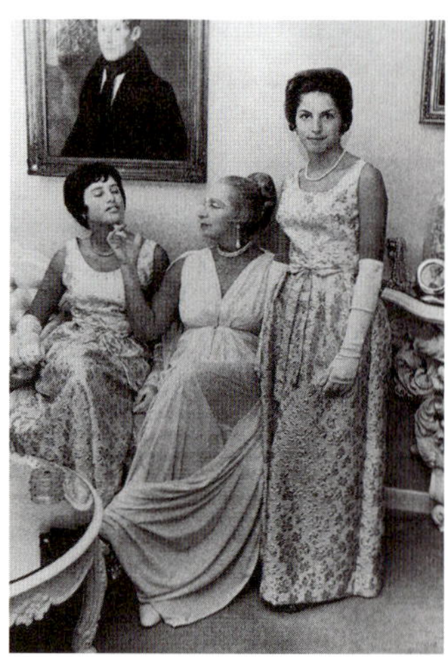

Coinciding as it did with the end of her artistic career, his death had a disastrous effect on her psyche. The last years of her life were particularly difficult for her daughter, Kizette, who had followed Lempicka to America and had married and had children of her own. Lempicka's strong personality and her need to control everything did not diminish with age. Following the death of her husband, the artist moved to Houston to be nearer her daughter and grandchildren. In 1978, she moved to Mexico, and continued to harass her family from there, changing her will countless times in a bid to persuade Kizette to look after not only her sick husband but also her elderly mother. Tamara de Lempicka died in 1980. Her daughter overcame all manner of bureaucratic red tape to fulfil her final wish: for her ashes to be scattered over the volcano Popocatépetl. ❖

Lempicka in Tres Bambus, Cuernavaca, Mexico, *c.* 1979

Lempicka with the topaz given to her by Gabriele d'Annunzio after their intended affair failed to take off, *c.* 1979

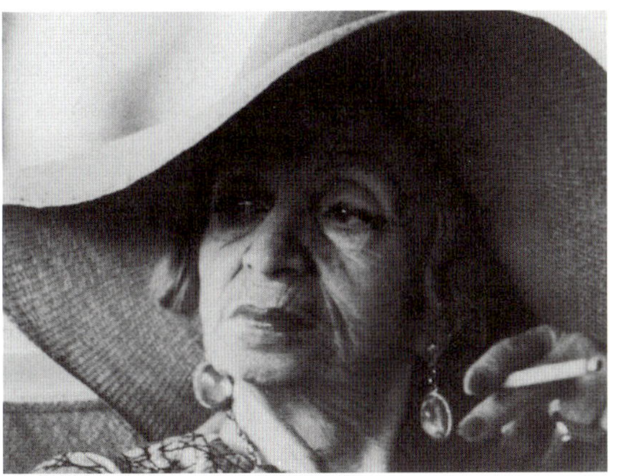

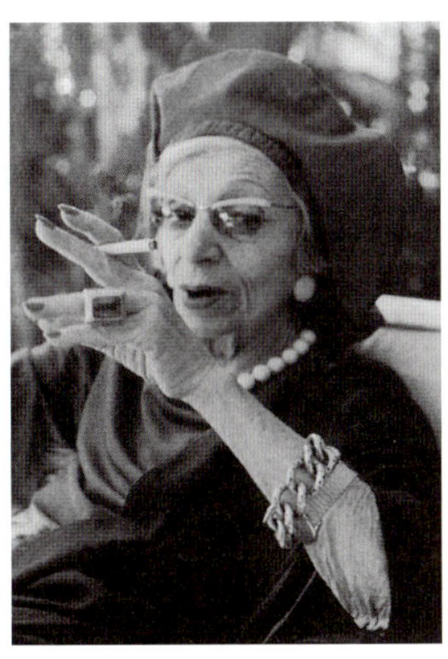

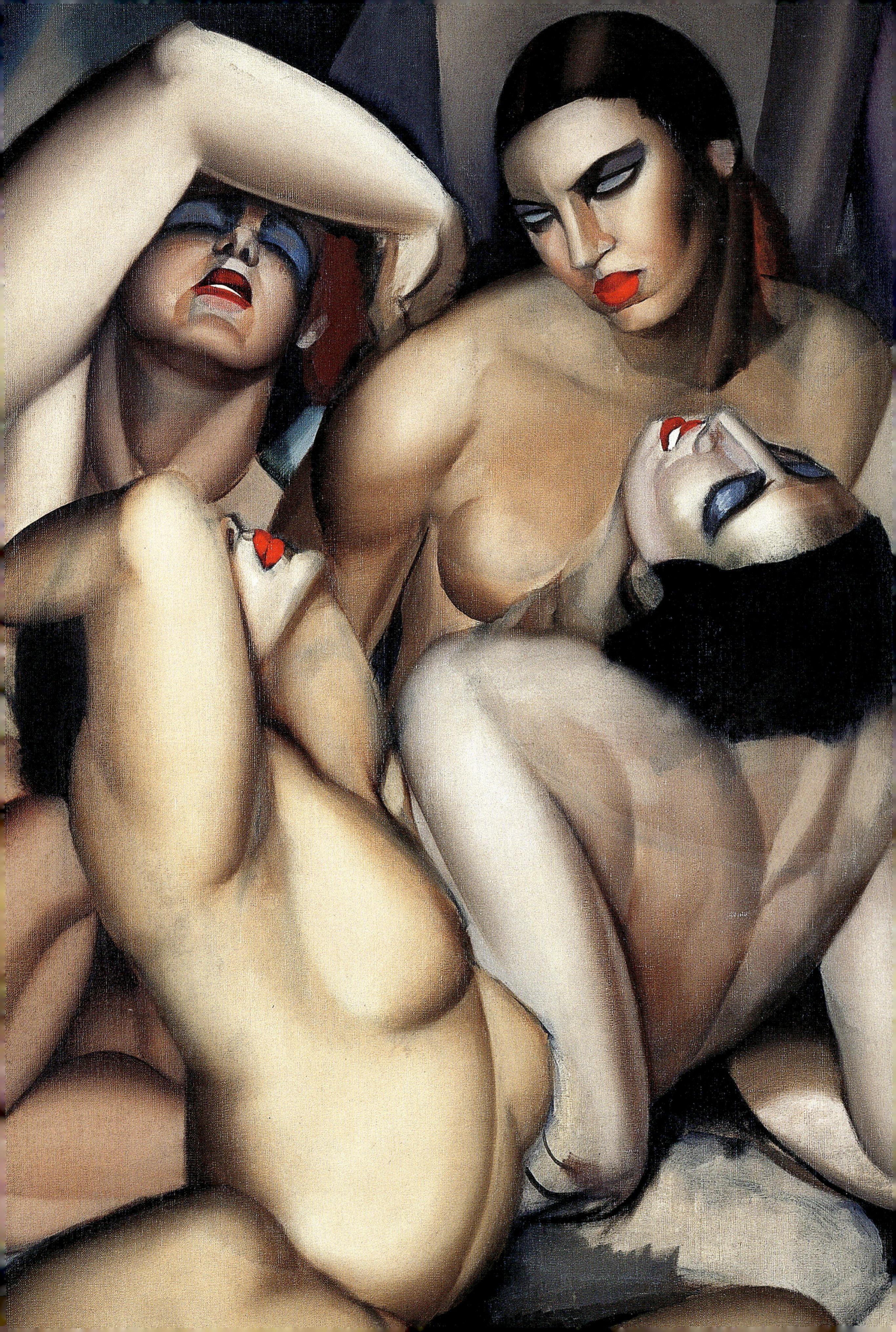

Plates

Ninety per cent of Tamara de Lempicka's work of the 1920s consists of portraits. The rest takes the form of still lifes, cityscapes and abstract works which are not dealt with here. Nature and landscape are mere background in her paintings, the artist's interest lying clearly in portraying the human individual.

No less than three quarters of her portraits are of women – alone, in pairs, modestly clothed, in evening gowns, half undressed or nude. The remaining quarter of her portraits show men who, unlike her female sitters, are almost all named. Most of these men were her lovers, albeit some of them only briefly. The men are portrayed in a similar manner to the women – their feminine eroticism and strangely distorted poses lend them an androgynous air. Towards the end of the Twenties, this style changed and the men tended to be portrayed standing, demonstrating their professional qualification and their social position of power. The Cubist influence in Lempicka's early paintings becomes increasingly diluted and her visual syntax cooler, smoother and more self-contained.

Perspective (Two Friends) 1923

In the early 1920s, Lempicka frequented the salons of Parisian society, including that of the American writer Natalie Barney – surely one of the most prominent lesbians in Paris apart from Gertrude Stein. Her salon, dedicated to Sappho, the goddess of love, attracted the literary and artistic greats of the day – James Joyce, Jean Cocteau, Thornton Wilder, Isadora Duncan, Paul Poiret and Colette – who undoubtedly enjoyed more than just the intellectual stimulation of the evening. André Gide, a regular guest of Barney, made an impression on Lempicka and they soon became friends. In 1923, Lempicka introduced Gide to Lhote, and both of them urged her to show *Perspective* at the Salon d'Automne. The blend of classical and contemporary vocabulary, together with the clearly homoerotic theme, quickly made this picture well-known. It was later purchased by the Musée d'art moderne in Geneva.

Oil on canvas, 130 × 160 cm, Musée d'art moderne, Petit Palais, Geneva

Two female nudes sit slightly off-centre. One rests her hand on the inside of the reclining figure's thigh. The figures form a triangle within an undefined room, with the urban architectural elements so typical of Lempicka in the background. A curtain at the left-hand edge of the picture heightens the spectator's voyeuristic pleasure in looking at the almost geometrically formed curves of these two women, who seem to oscillate between the emotional coldness of their almost aggressive nudity and the demonstrative sensuality of their pose. The reduced palette of greys and greens is accentuated only by the bright red lips of the women.

André Gide, c. 1925. Oil on cardboard, 50 × 35 cm, private collection

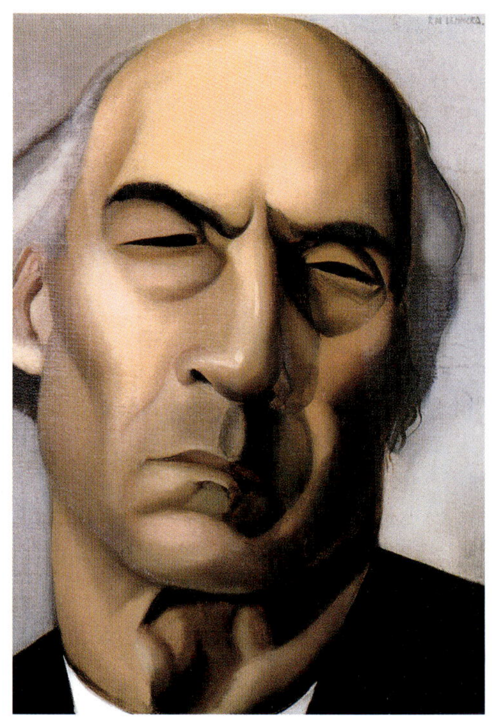

36

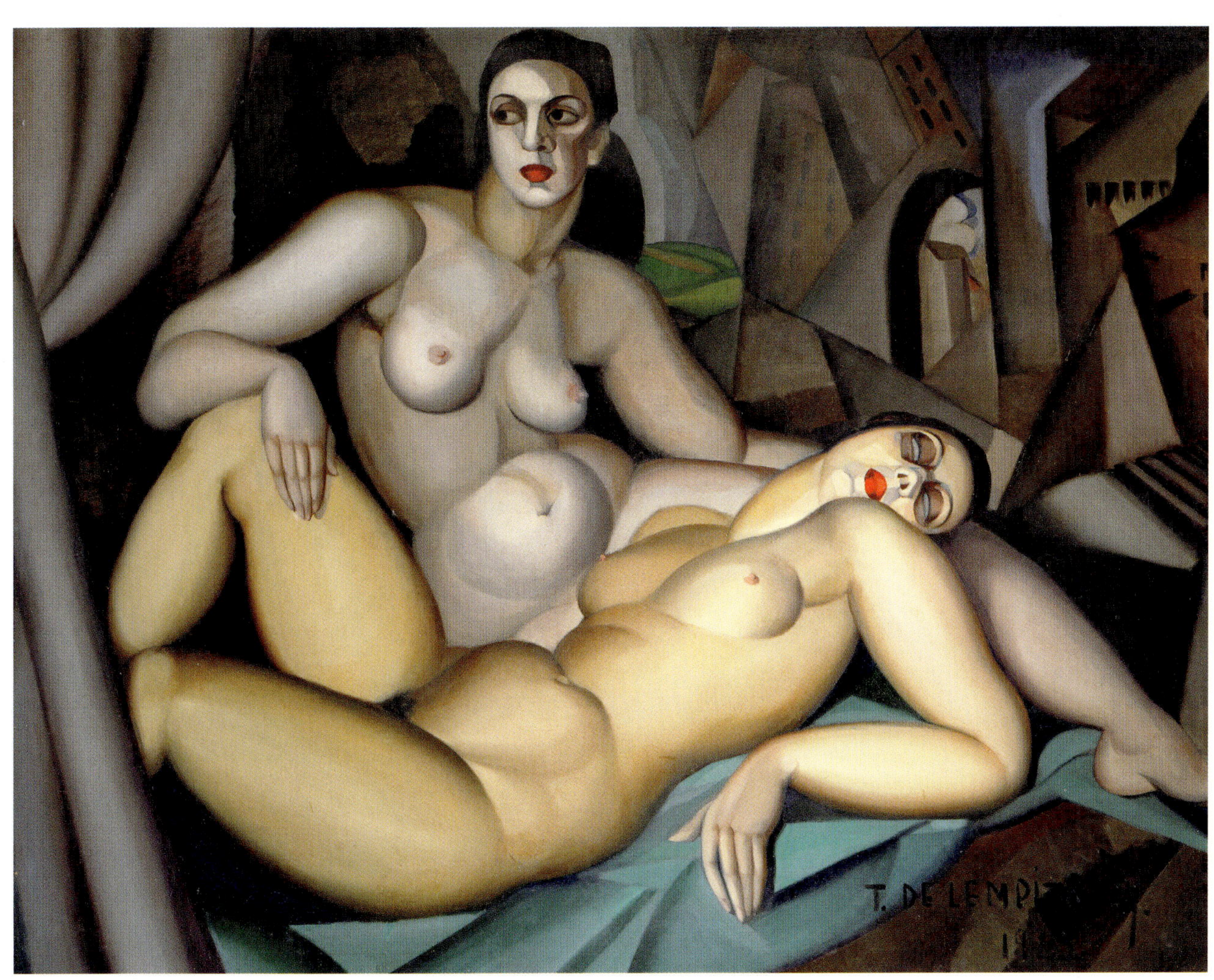
T. DE LEMPI

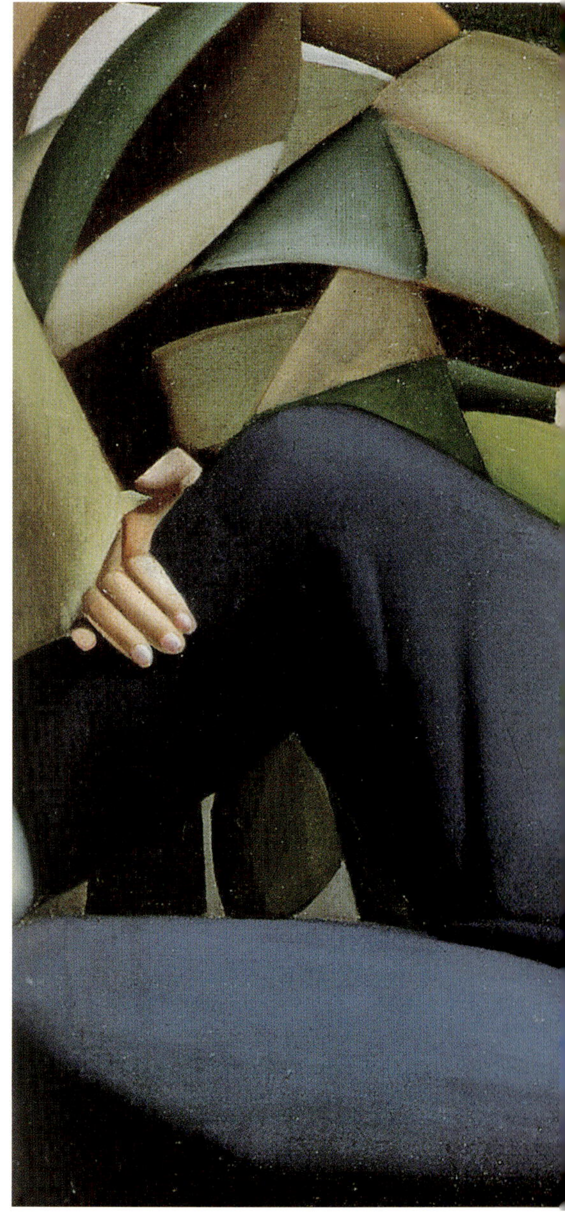

"I had always innamorato, always. For my inspiration,
I liked to go out in the evenings and have a good-
looking man tell me how beautiful I am or how great
an artist I am – and he touches my hand … I loved it!
I needed that. And I had many, many."[12]

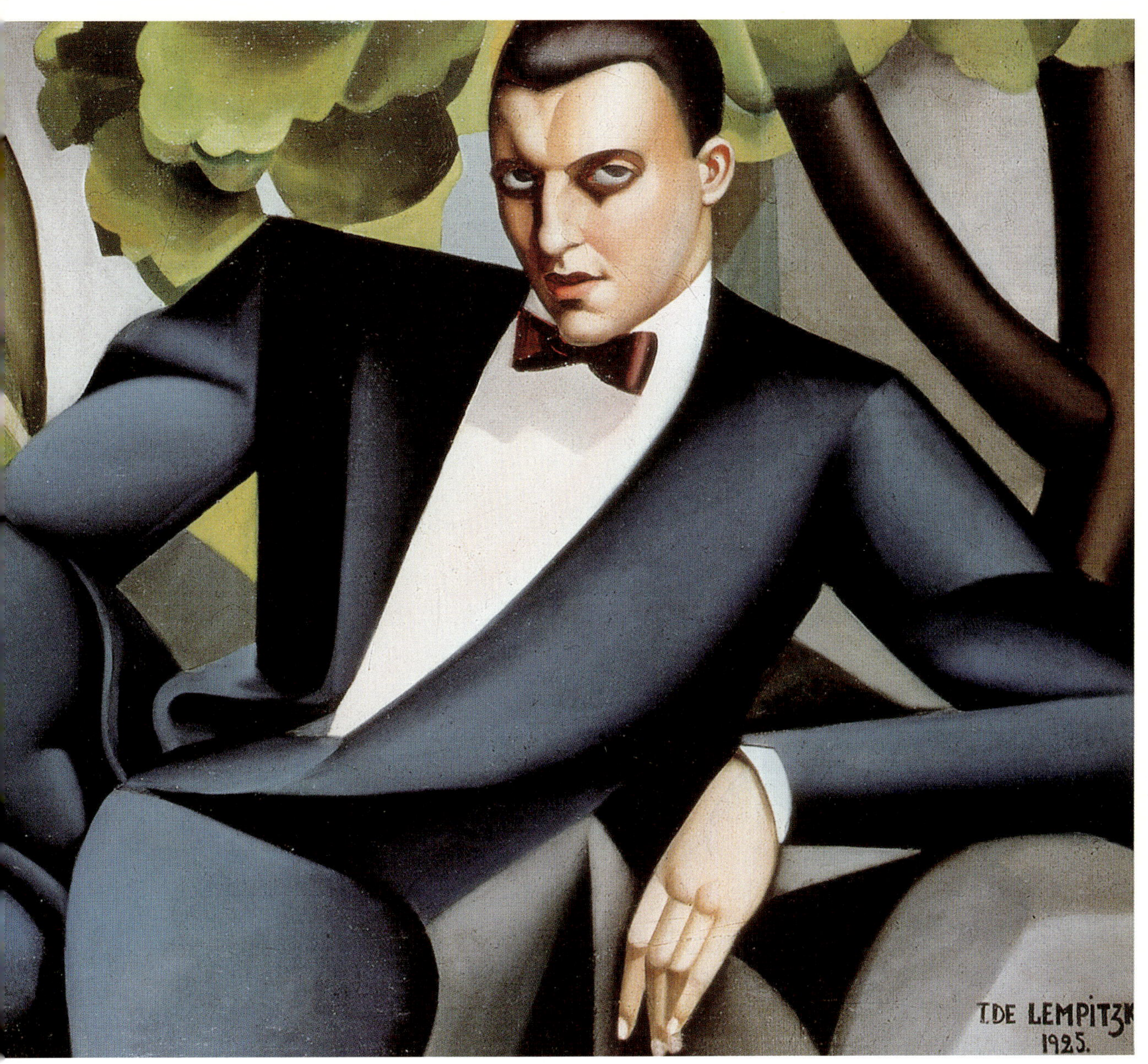
T. DE LEMPITZKI
1925.

Portrait of the Duchess de La Salle   1925

The viewer is confronted by an almost life-size portrait of the Duchess de la Salle. She stands before us in riding gear, her tailored shirt open, her hair fashionably bobbed, her pose both casual and elegant – a modern, sporting woman. But there is an element of coquettishness in her appearance that contradicts the character of the portrait. It is painted in the tradition of the classic swagger portrait with the usual attributes of power, such as the red carpet, the curtain and the column in the background.

Oil on canvas, 162 × 97 cm, Wolfgang Joop Collection, Hamburg

The way the Duchess tilts her head slightly to one side, with a hint of melancholy in her challenging gaze, is not something we might expect to find in a typical aristocratic portrait. Between the curtain and the column, a cityscape can be glimpsed. To right of the curtain there is a patch of blue sky. The Duchess seems to be in charge of this grey, Cubist landscape, dominating the space with her confident, masculine, authoritarian body language. The dark violet of her bob and her emphatically casual pose might be an indication of her origins in the world of prostitution.

Just as her female forms are concealed beneath her masculine garb and pose, so too is her possible profession merely hinted at: take, for example, the way the supporting right leg is clothed in a loose-fitting swathe of fabric, while the left leg, bent towards us, is covered in skin-tight material and our attention is drawn to this by the gesture of her hand. The way the pelvic area becomes the focus of the picture suggests that Lempicka wanted to portray her sitter as the unconventional and self-assured mistress of her own desires. She did not paint a 'real' duchess (the title and the name de La Salle are probably freely invented), but the 'Babylonian whore' – a metaphor often associated with Paris at the time, particularly in literature. With her monumental *Portrait of the Duchess de La Salle*, the artist presents a new female image, demonstrating an

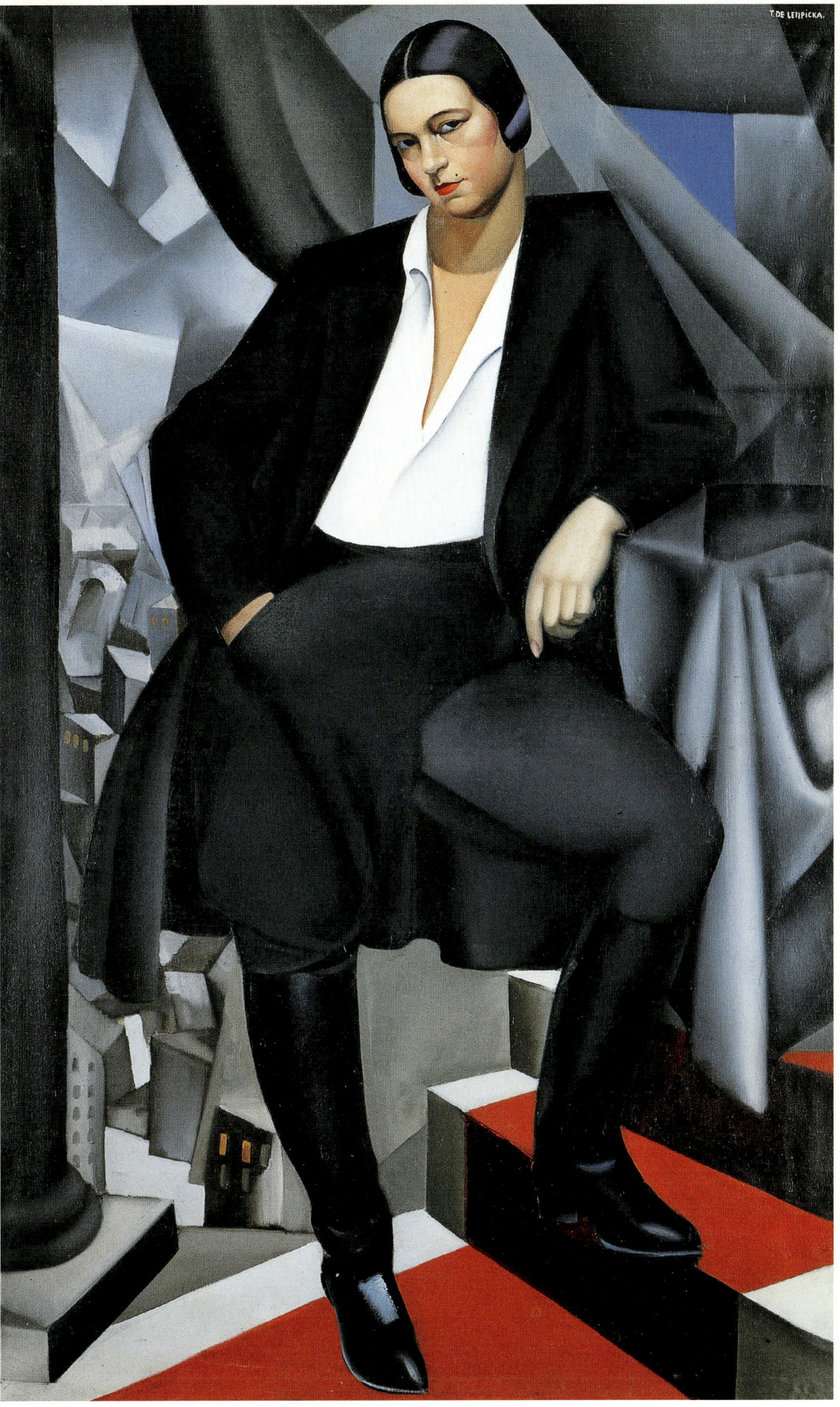

T.DE LEMPICKA.

active approach to physicality and sexuality. Women wearing trousers only gradually gained acceptance in the Twenties, mainly through horse-riding, but in the everyday world of work and socialising, they were still taboo. A 1925 article on 'women in recent art' disparagingly notes: "In summer, she sportingly plays tennis and golf, she pretends to be interested in riding, she goes to the mountains, she rows and sails. In winter, she skis and bobsleighs and toboggans. Every sporting activity is identified in her mind with the opportunity of casually encountering the opposite sex and the quest for sexual excitement. She only goes in for sexual sport, and just as she makes sexuality a sport, so too does sport become sexuality for her."[13]

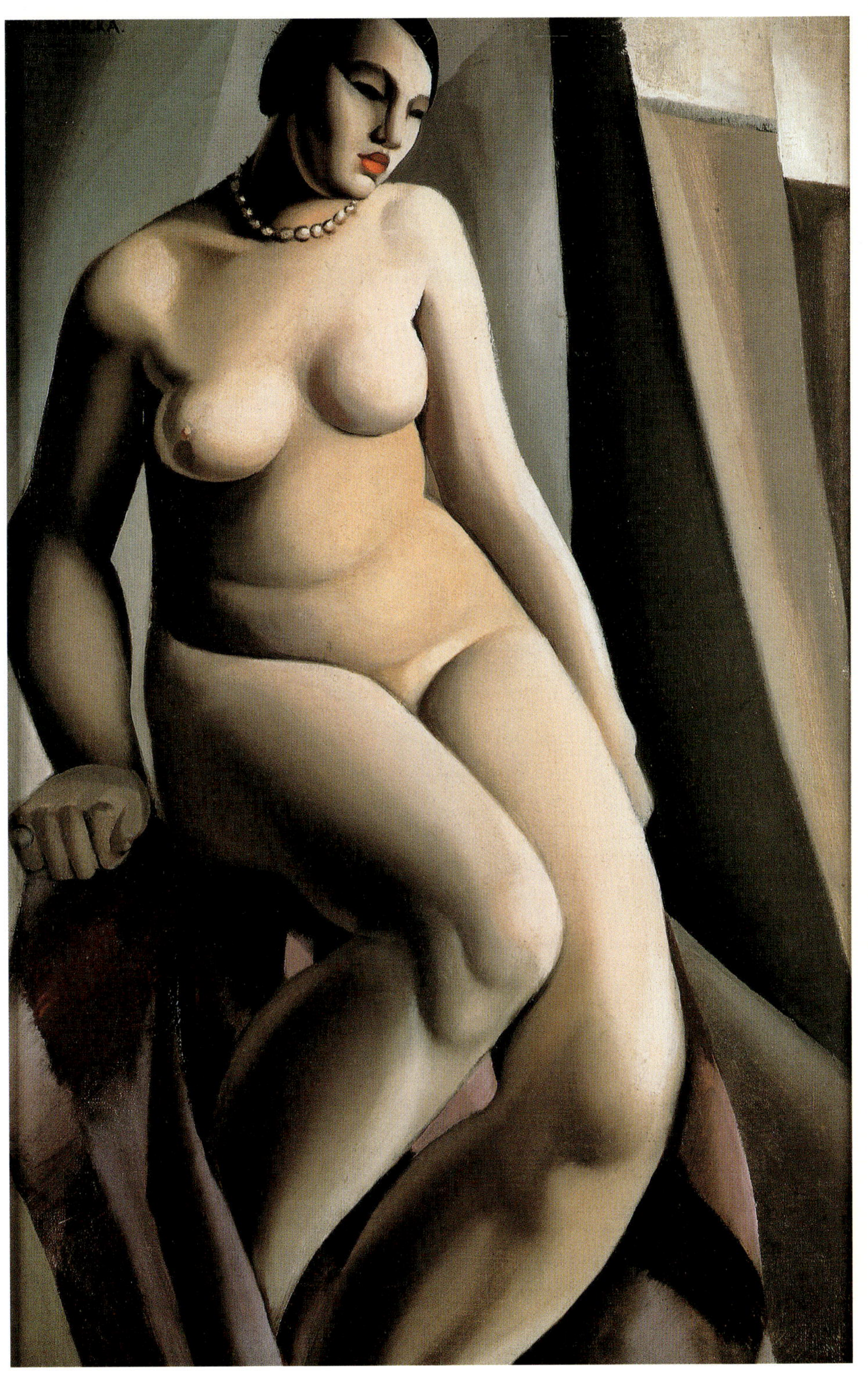

Seated Nude   1925

Oil on canvas, 61 × 38 cm,
private collection

The Model   1925

Most of Lempicka's models for her nude portraits were prosti-
tutes, whom she approached on the street or in cafés. The
artist may well not have known their names; if she did, she
chose not to divulge them. During these first years in Paris,
Lempicka was sexually adventurous, indulging her own homo-
sexual leanings at wild parties (the details of which she later
shared with various interviewers). *The Model* was painted during this phase, and is signed 'Lempitzki' – the masculine form
of her name which she hoped would temper any disadvan-
tages she might encounter in the art world as a woman.

In this painting, the classical training and the school of André
Lhote with its rhythmic forms are clearly in evidence. Superficially conventional as this painting may seem, it nevertheless plays with traditional forms, achieving a distinctive
harmony and balance of movement and colour. The right arm
covers much of the face, notably the eyes, while the left hand
grasps the flimsy slip, pulling it up so that the heavy thigh is
even more prominent in the foreground. The model is flanked
on either side by S-curved strips of black. These, together with
the modestly covered eyes, suggest a view through a keyhole
and joyful anticipation of what is soon to be discovered. They
foreshadow her later perfection in reducing the spectator to
the role of voyeur.

Oil on canvas, 116 × 73 cm,
private collection

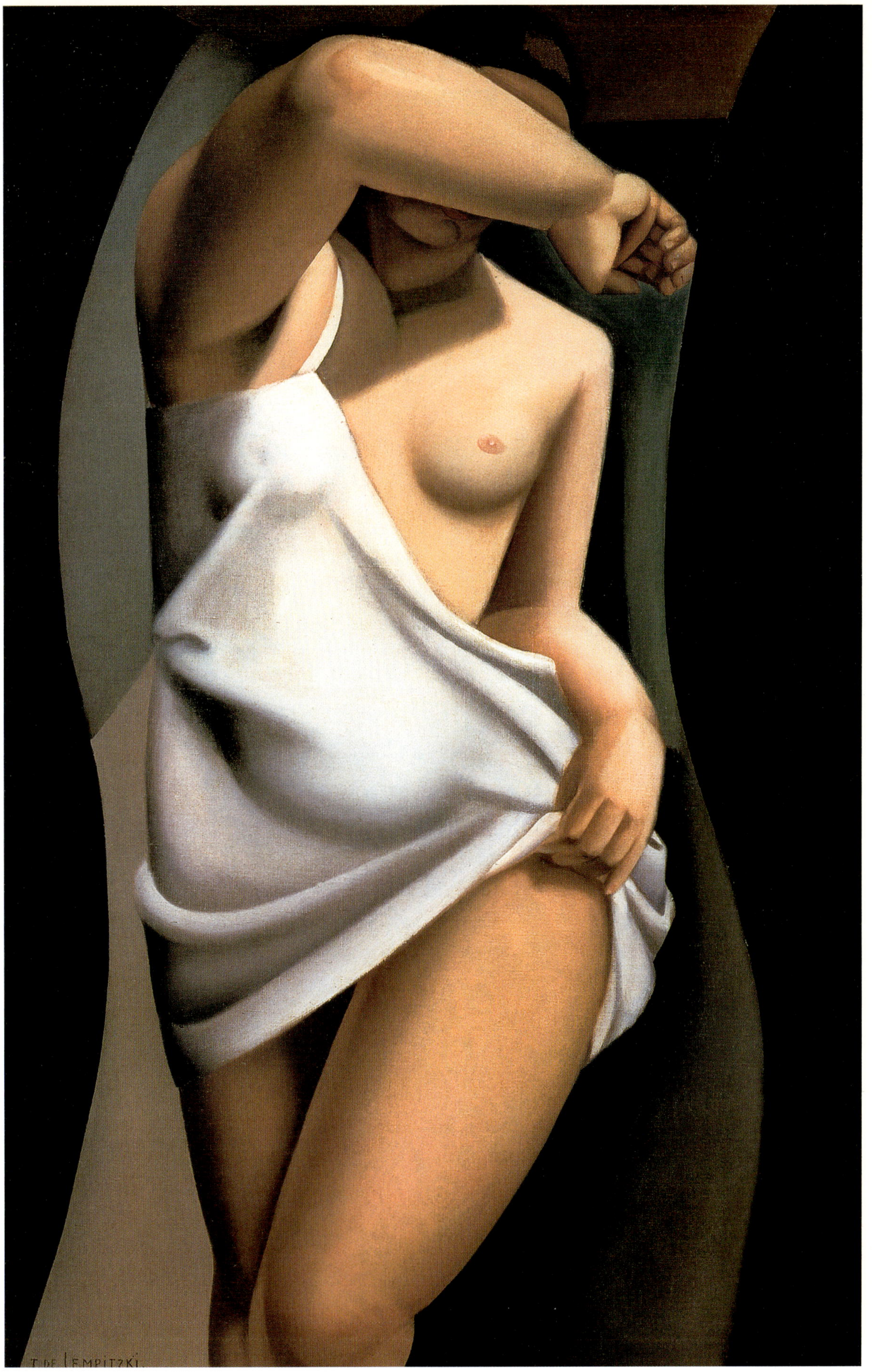

T. DE LEMPITZKI

Beautiful Rafaela   1927

This female nude is unusual for Lempicka in that the format is horizontal. The figure is reclining in an audacious pose that emphasises her voluptuous forms. Her black hair, dark red, slightly opened lips and closed eyes underline the sense of lasciviousness, which is heightened still further by the position of the right hand with its fingertips touching her breast. There are few colours in this painting; only the bright red accentuates the browns and blacks and is echoed in the cloth covering the woman's feet, in the lips, and in an undefined red area at the lower right. Beautiful Rafaela was discovered by the artist on one of her strolls through the Bois de Boulogne. According to Lempicka, she was "the most beautiful woman I have ever seen – huge black eyes, beautiful sensuous mouth, beautiful body." She took the girl home with her and painted portraits of her over a period of more than a year. It is quite probable that she was a prostitute. The painting was exhibited at the Salon d'Automne, where it immediately drew attention, but did not trigger any extreme reactions. It was not until fifty years later that an article in the *Sunday Times* described it as one of the most important nudes of the twentieth century.

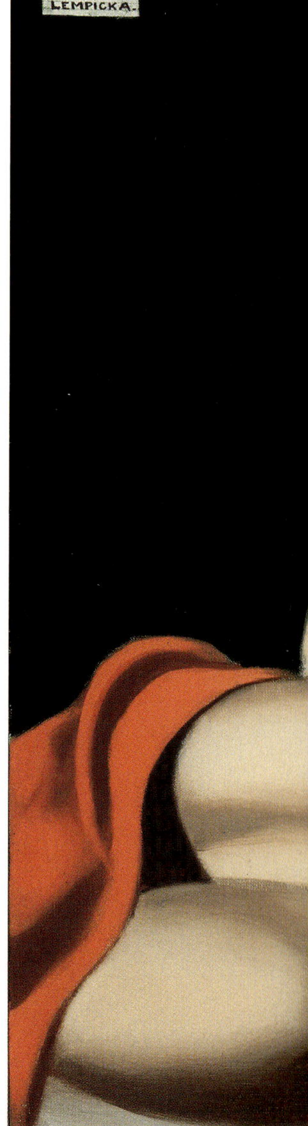

Oil on canvas, 64 × 91 cm,
private collection

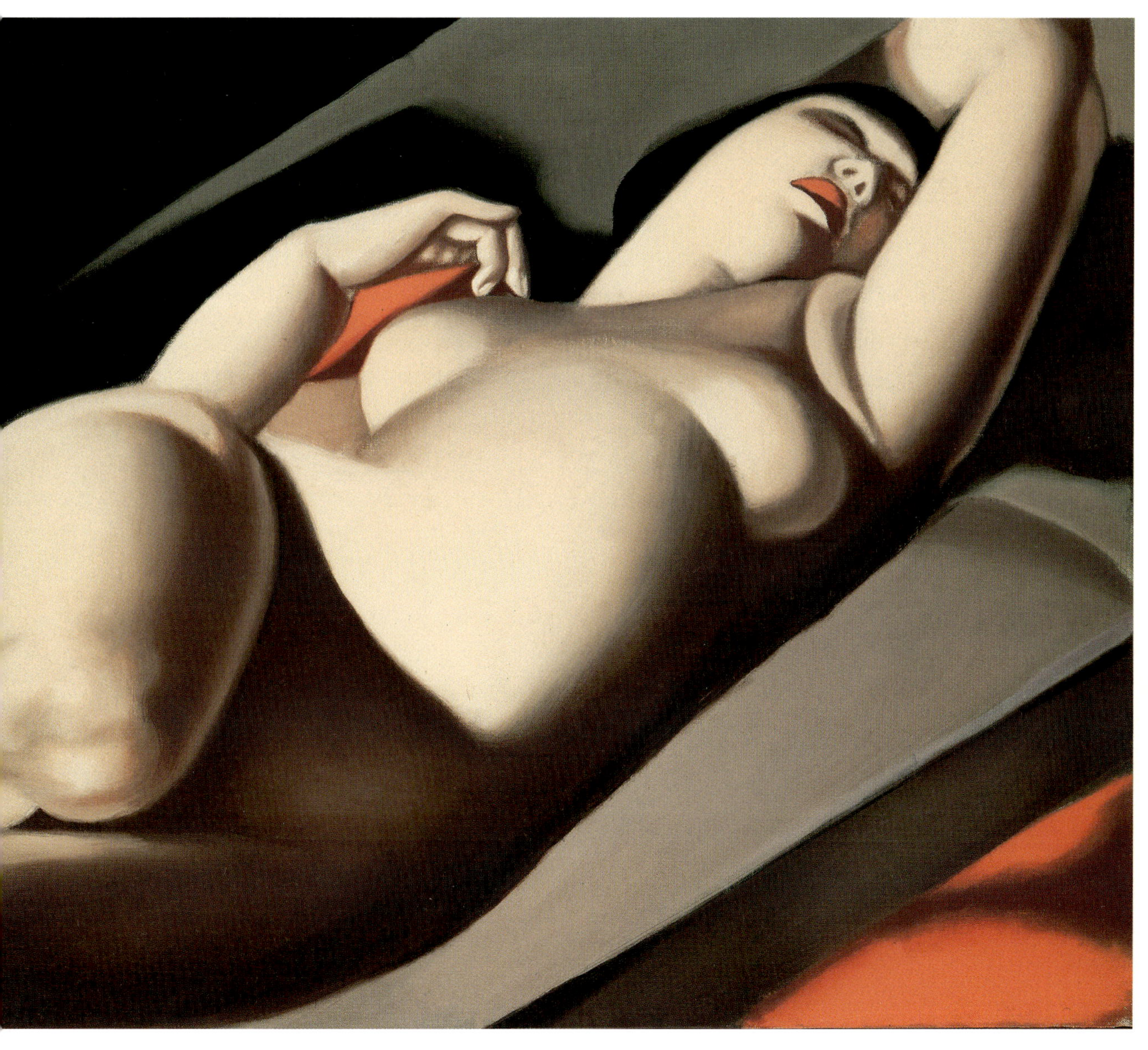

The Dream   1927

Oil on canvas, 81 × 60 cm,
private collection

Also known as *Rafaela with Green Background*, this dreamy
nude is a far cry from the hard, cold atmosphere of many of
the artist's portraits.

"Every one of my paintings
is a self-portrait."[14]

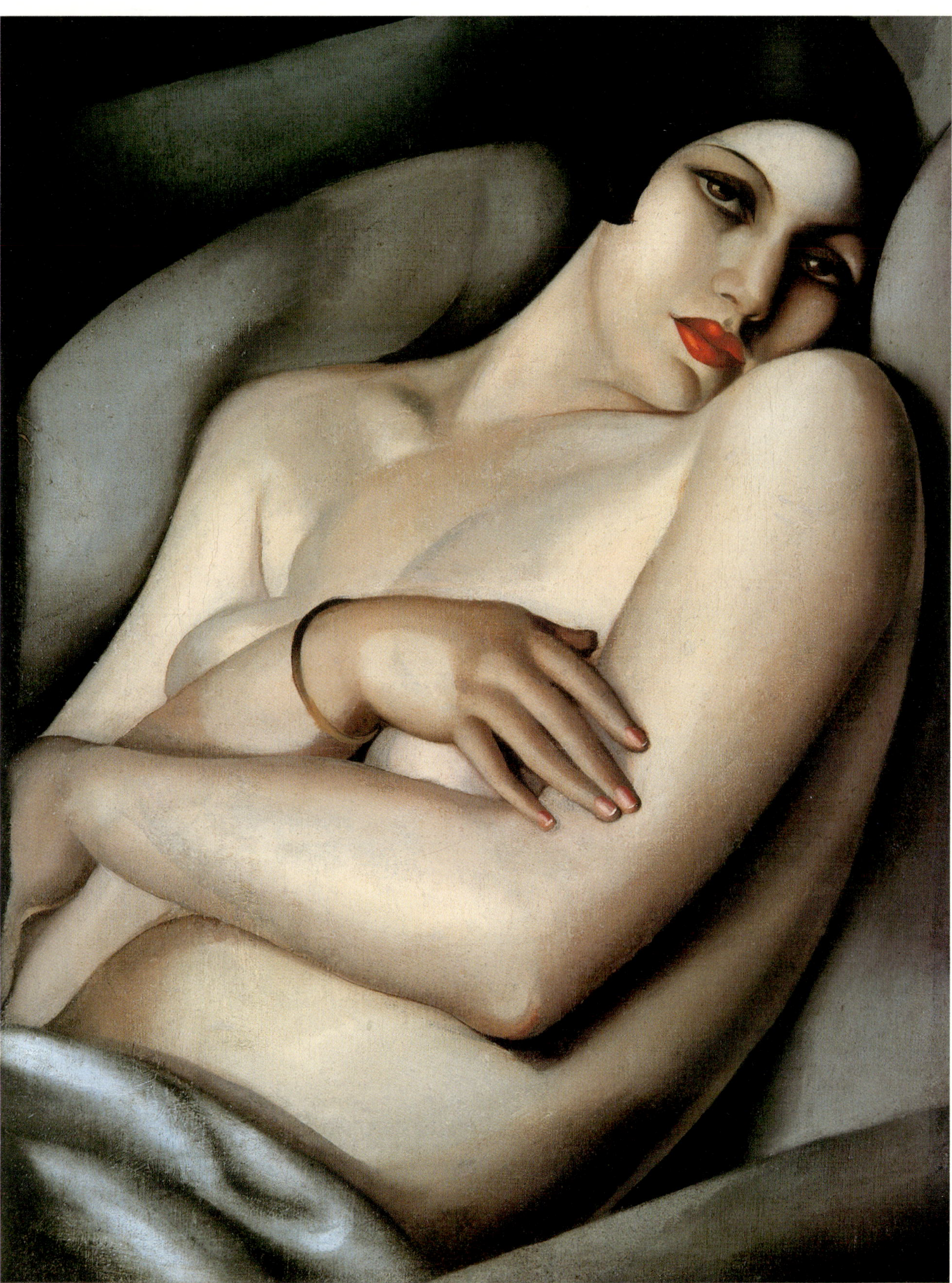

Portrait of His Imperial Highness Grand Duke Gabriel   1927

Oil on canvas, 116 × 65 cm,
private collection

"She was only interested in people whom she called 'the best':
the rich, the powerful and the successful … She hated
everything that was middle-class, average or just 'nice'." [15]

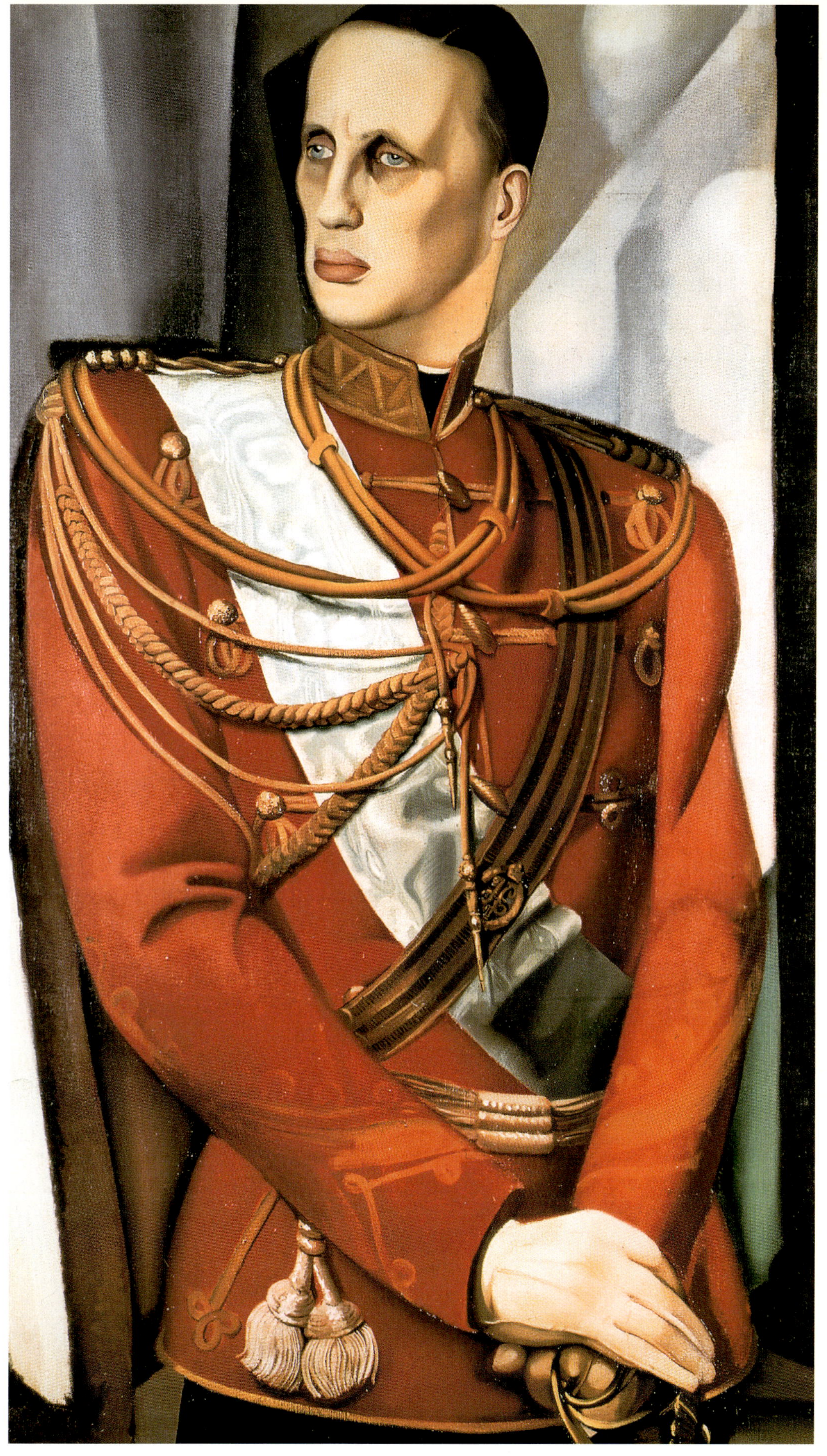

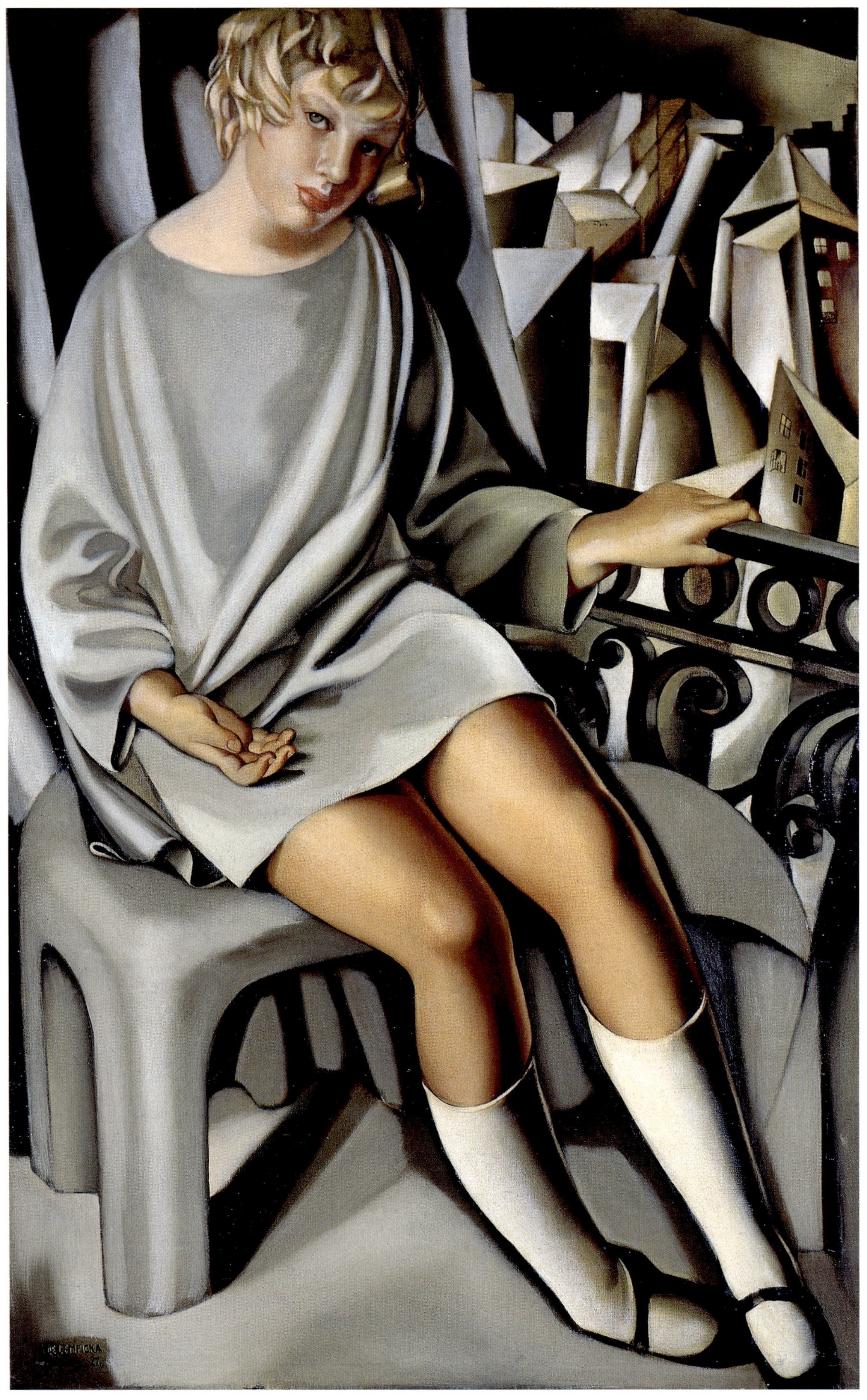

Oil on canvas, 126 × 82 cm,
Musée national d'art moderne,
Paris

Pouting but at the same time proud of her task of sitting as model once more for her powerful mother, Kizette is seated on a chair on a balcony wearing only a short dress, white knee socks and black shoes. Her left hand, resting on the railing, points towards the geometric architectural elements in the background. Although it is her own daughter she is painting here, Lempicka does not shy from portraying an underlying sense of sexual awakening. The naive gaze, the pouting lips and the short dress all call the apparent innocence of the model into question.

This painting, predominantly in greys and greens, took first prize at the Exposition Internationale des Beaux-Arts in Bordeaux in 1927, confirming to the artist that she was moving in the right direction. In the years that followed, Kizette would often act as her mother's model. In spite of all their conflicts, she was glad to do so, for it was the only way of spending a little more time with her mother – even though the artist treated her daughter with the same impersonal professionalism as she treated any other model during the sittings.

Ira Perrot was, for many years, the artist's neighbour and best friend and sat as her model for many portraits. Alexander Chodkieweitz, who knew Lempicka in her early Paris years and who has been able to confirm details of many of her acquaintances, reported that Lempicka always spoke with awe of Ira's supple figure and her magnificent breasts. Here, Lempicka portrays her model in a white dress accentuated only by the folds of a carefully draped stole. In her right arm she is cradling some white calla lilies, which are arranged as if in a still life. The background disappears almost completely behind the metallic coolness of these forms.

Oil on wood, 99 × 65 cm, private collection

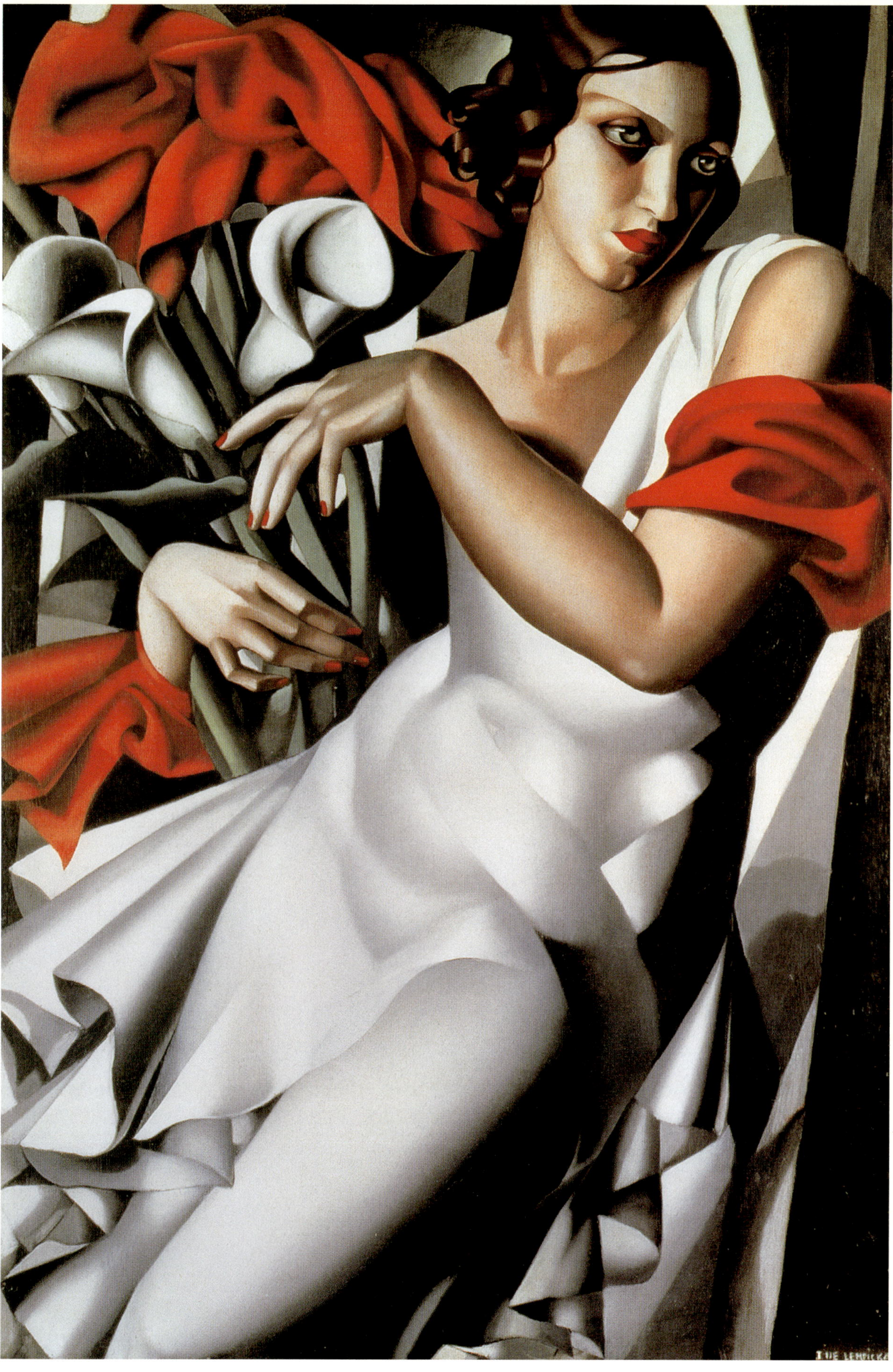

Portrait of Romana de la Salle   1928

Oil on canvas, 162 × 97 cm,
Wolfgang Joop Collection,
Hamburg

"I looked for a *métier* that did not exist
any longer … I aimed at technique, *métier*,
simplicity, and good taste. My goal: do not
copy. Create a new style, colours light and
bright, return to elegance in my models."[16]

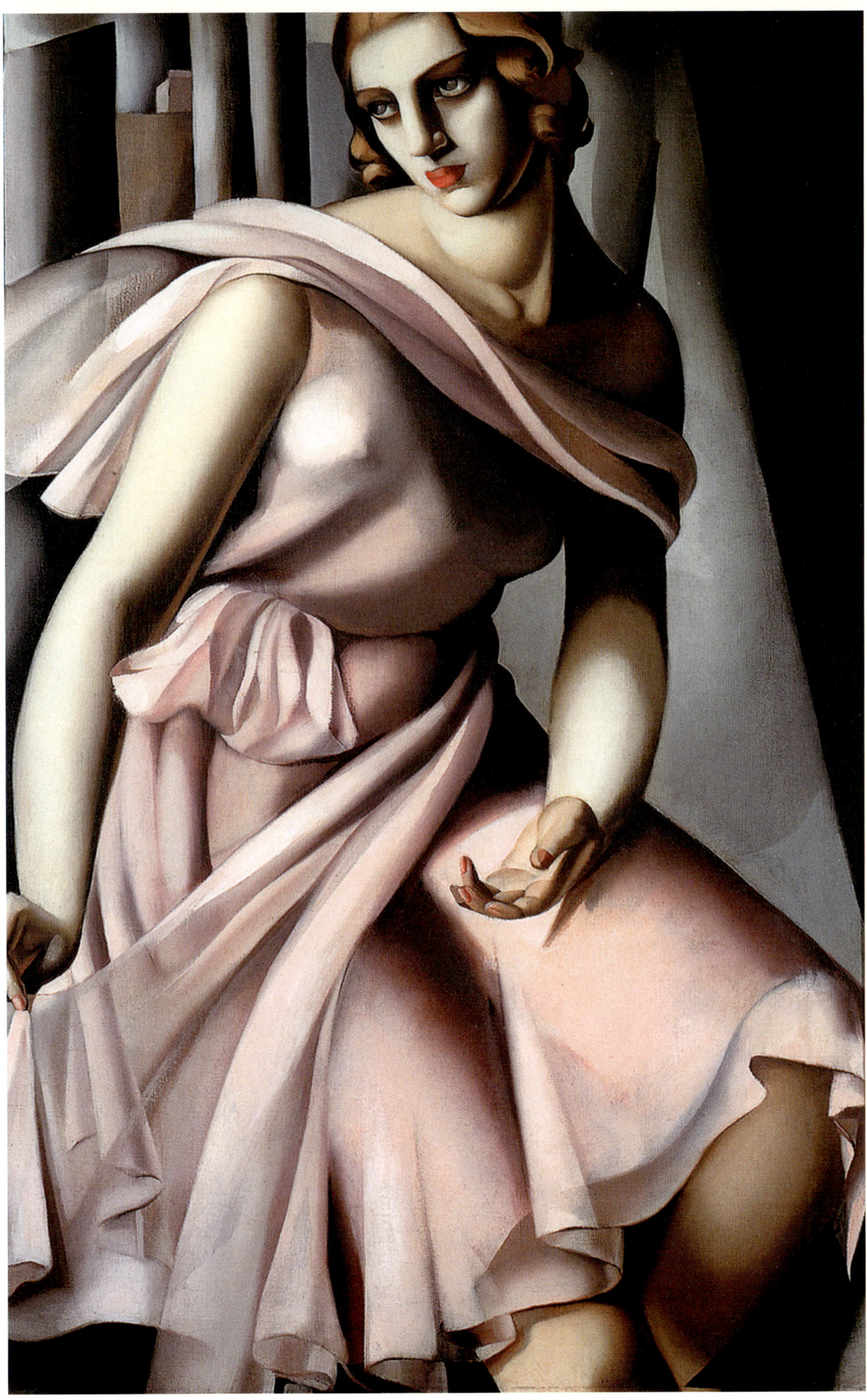

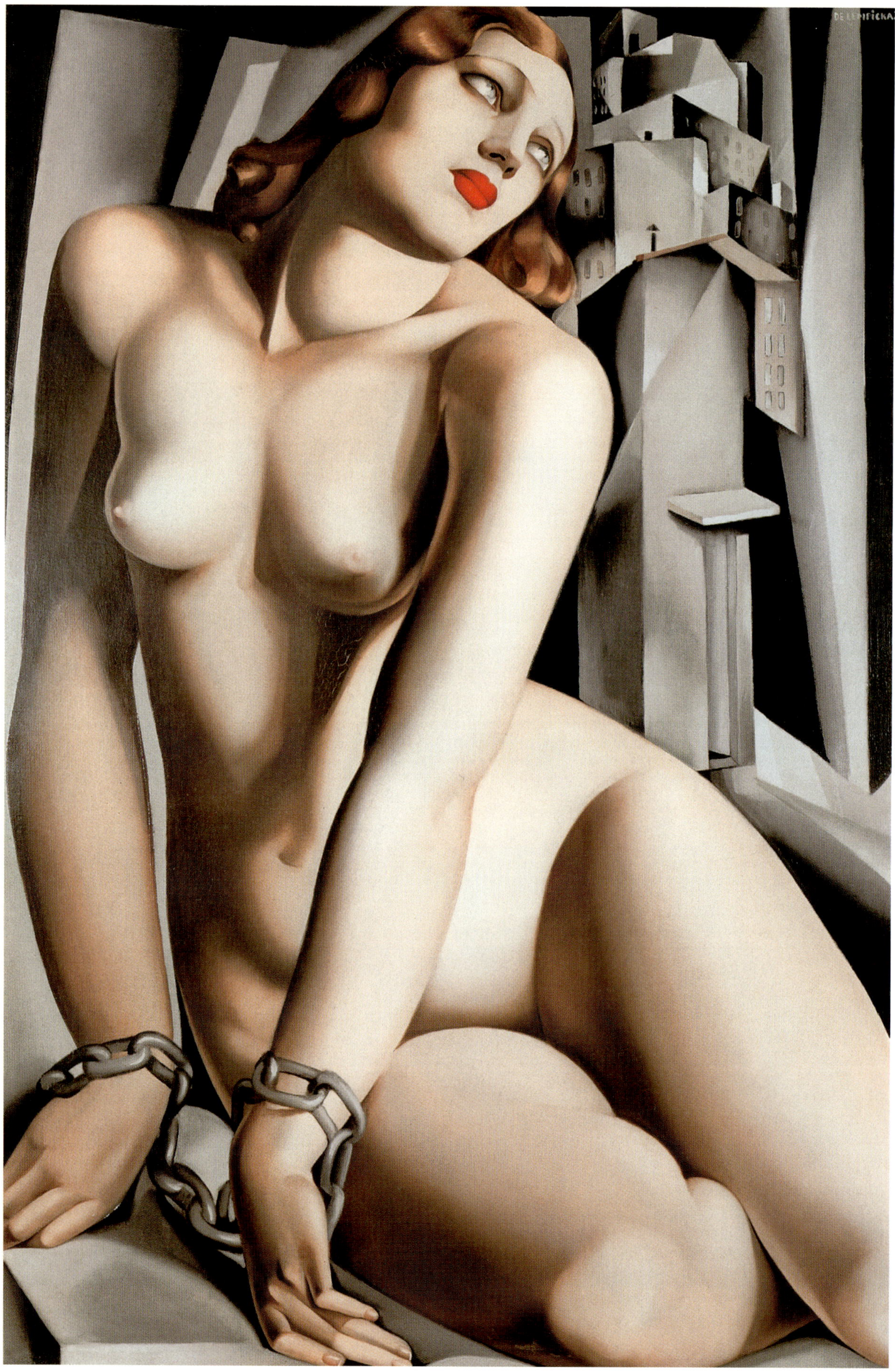

Andromeda 1927/28

Oil on canvas, 99 × 65 cm,
private collection

In Greek mythology, Andromeda was the daughter of Cepheus, King of Ethiopia, and Cassiopeia. As punishment for Cassiopeia's vanity in considering herself more beautiful than the Nereids, Poseidon sent the sea monster Cetus and unleashed a deluge. In order to deliver the country from the monster, Andromeda was chained to a cliff as a sacrifice to Cetus. She was freed by Perseus, who married her. Lempicka transposes this Greek myth to the urban setting of her 1920s paintings. A brunette nude gazing heavenwards fills almost the entire frame. Her hands are chained, and in the background are the typical urban architectural elements. The beautiful woman seems to be awaiting her fate. This is a picture that clearly reflects the ideas of her teacher Lhote and his own admiration for the school of Ingres. Ingres's heroines have at times been described as thick-necked, and Lempicka's Andromeda also has this feature, indicative of a thyroid malfunction which, it was formerly believed, made women more sexually active. The similarity with Ingres's Angélique, right down to the twist of the body, is certainly striking.

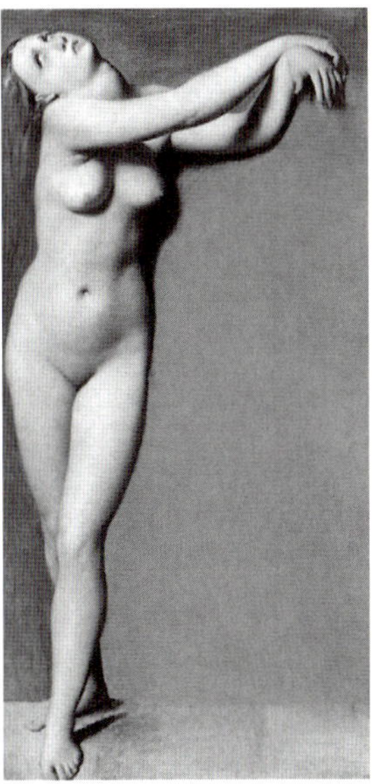

Jean Auguste Dominique Ingres, study for *Roger and Angélique*, 1819. Oil on canvas, 84.5 x 42.5 cm, Musée du Louvre, Paris

Self-Portrait (Tamara in the Green Bugatti)   1929

An extremely cropped view shows the artist herself looking out from her modern Bugatti at the surprised spectator with a self-assured and challenging gaze. The picture is aloof and cool – an impression further heightened by the use of the then fashionable turquoise hue. At the same time, the sensuality of the mouth is so strongly emphasised by the bright red lipstick that it cannot fail to be the focus of our gaze. The somewhat disdainful glance through half-closed eyelids nips any comment about women and modern technology in the bud. She creates a fascinating symbiosis with the automobile, the ultimate vehicle for conveying the ambivalence between the masculine and the feminine – the two extremes between which Lempicka likes to move. The painting itself was done at the very time when the active modern woman had got out of the saddle and into the driving seat, though it was to be some time yet before these 'automobilised' women would be regarded by the general public with anything other than a mixture of concern and pity. Advertising, in particular, repeatedly warned women against excess of any kind 'in the interests of their beauty'. "One day in Monte Carlo – it must have been 1927 or 1928, no matter … I left my car to go into Chanel. It was my little Renault, not green, but bright yellow and black. When I drove in it, I wore a pullover of the same bright yellow, always with a black skirt and hat. I was dressed like the car and the car like me. When I *retourne* I find a note on the windscreen. No name, a message only. It said: 'You look so wonderful in the car I would like to meet you.'"[17] It turned out that the message had been left by the fashion *directrice* of the chic Berlin women's magazine *Die Dame*, who wanted Lempicka to do a painting of herself and her yellow car for the cover of the magazine. The picture was published as the cover of *Die Dame* in 1929 and was to be the first in a series of works commissioned for the magazine. Needless to say, Lempicka did not paint her little yellow Renault, but a big green Bugatti which she had never owned, but which perfectly suited the image she had of herself.

Oil on wood, 35 × 26 cm,
Renaud Collection, Basle

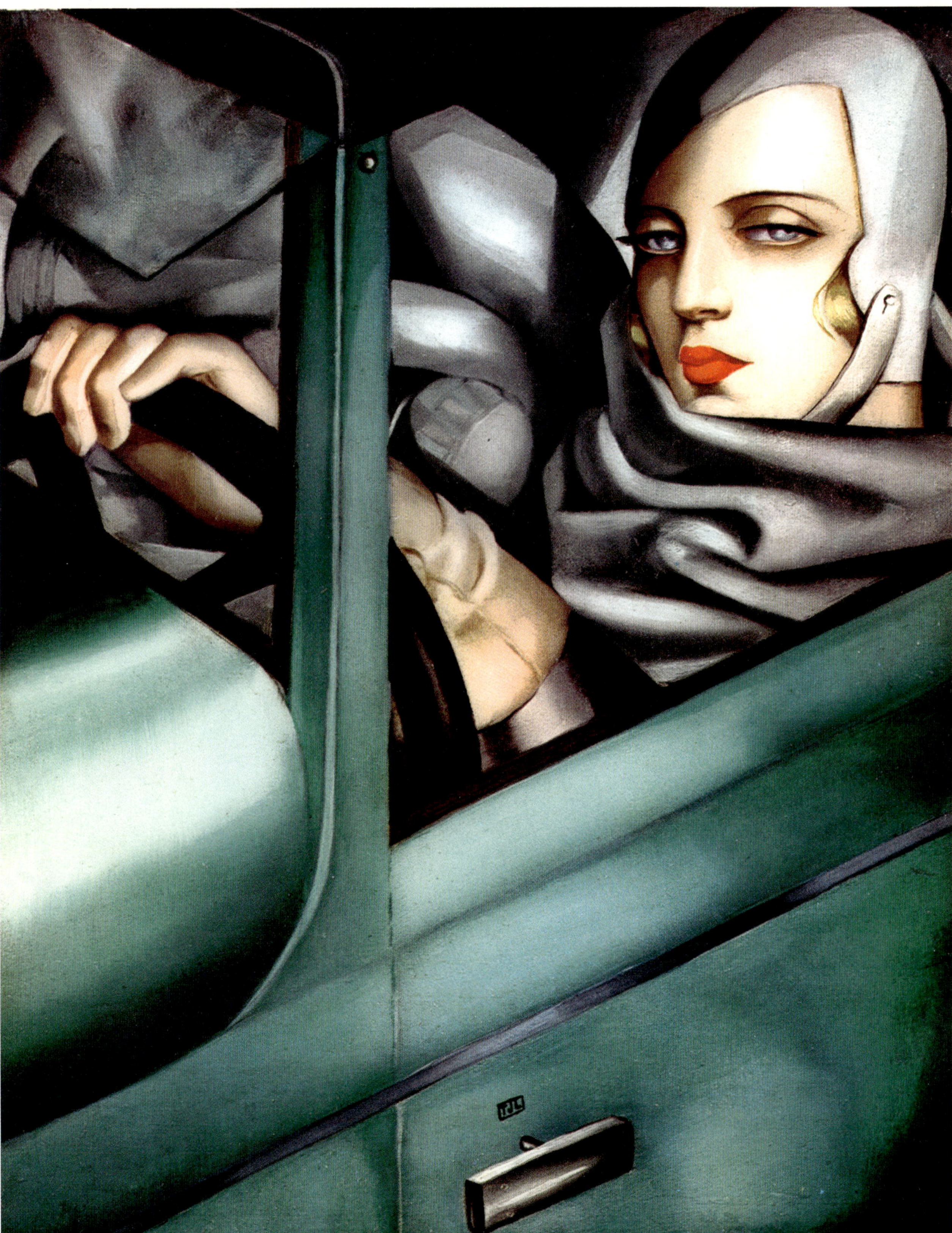

"I live life on the fringes of society
and the rules of normal society don't
apply on the fringes." [18]

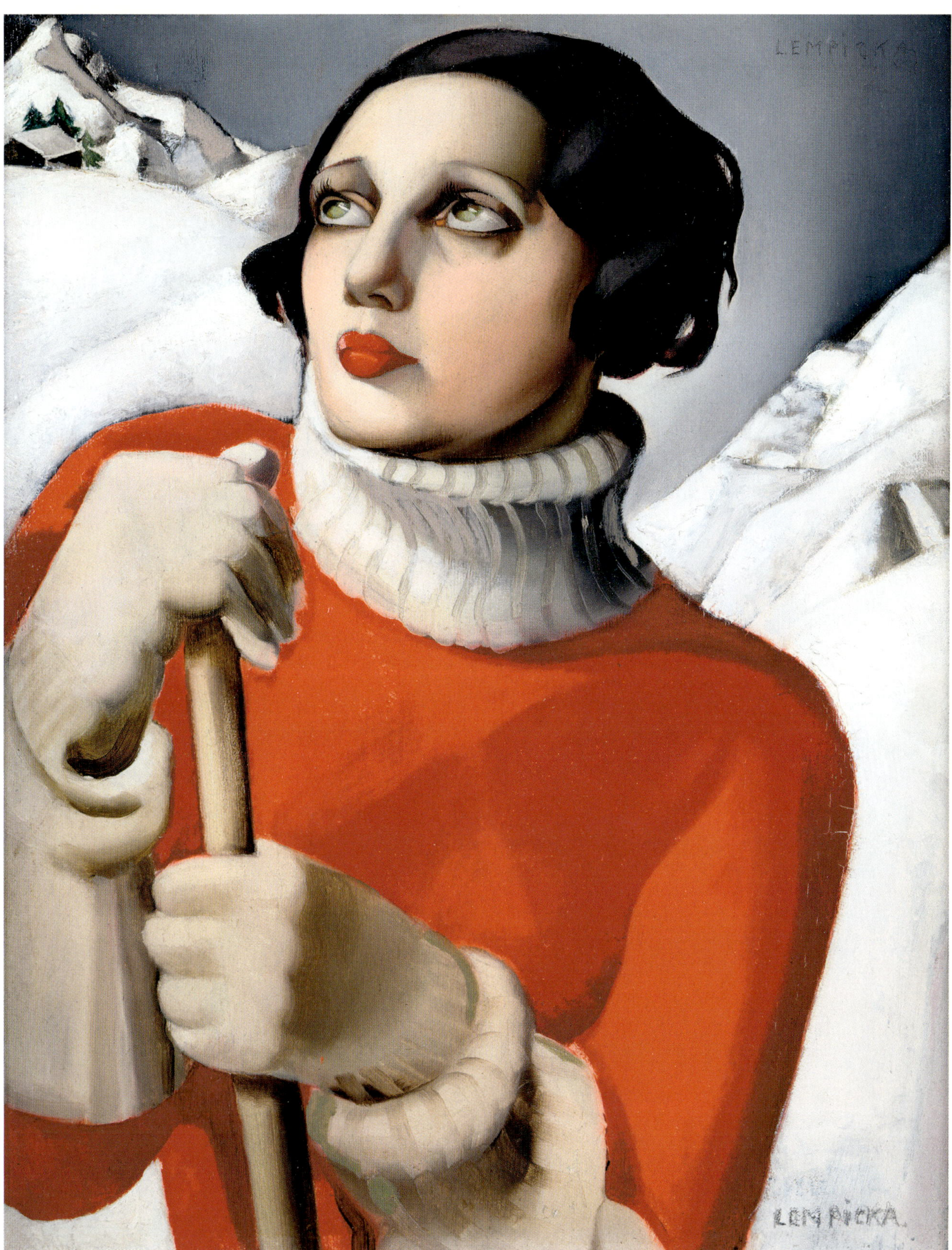

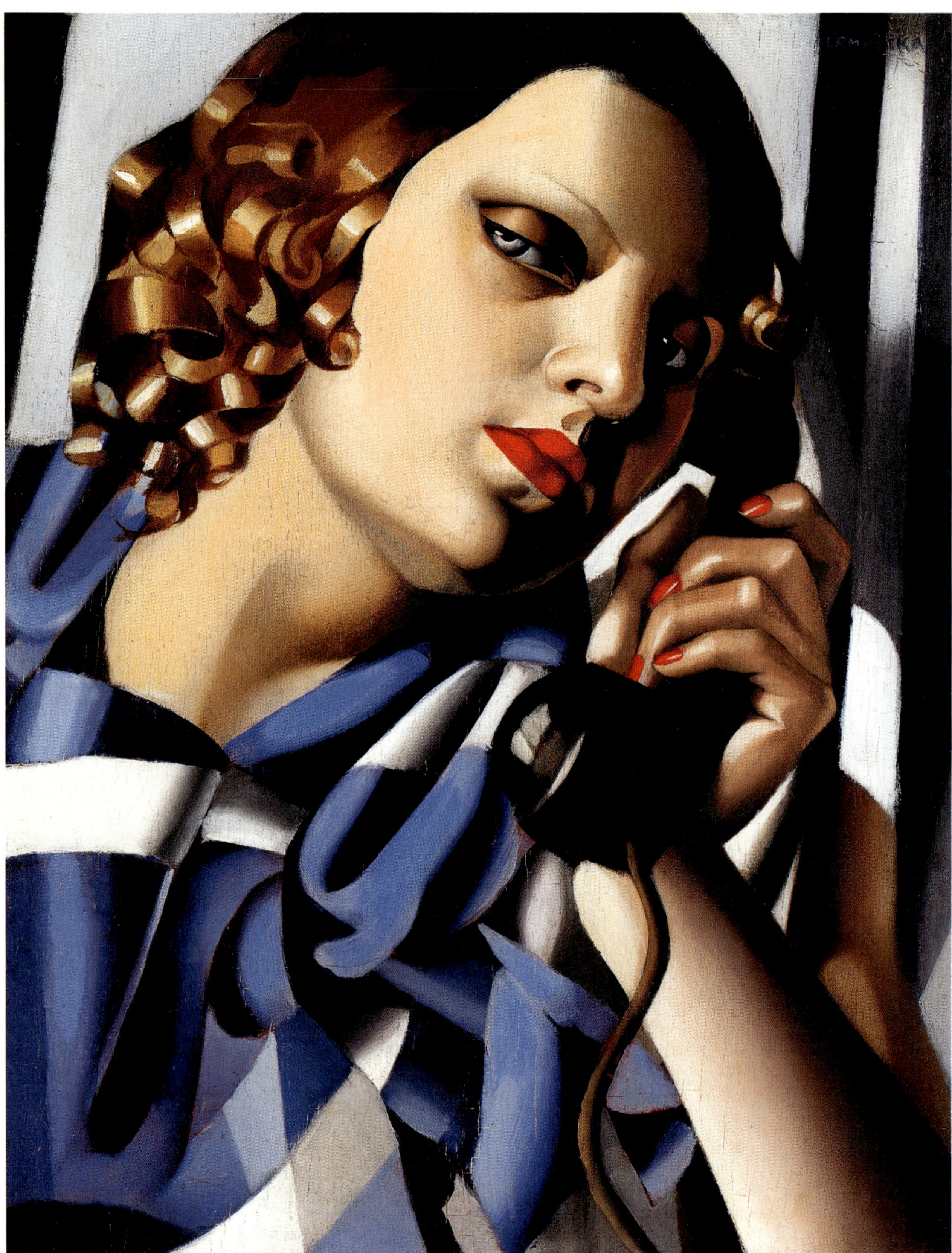

The Telephone II 1930

Oil on wood, 35 × 27 cm,
Wolfgang Joop Collection,
Hamburg

"My idea was always the best of the best.
Work was not enough. You had to have success.
Then you have money. Then you have the best
exhibitions, then they get the best newspaper
reviews, then you get everything that goes with
the best of the best."[19]

Tadeusz de Lempicki (unfinished)   1928

Even at the very height of her marital crisis, Lempicka made an attempt at reconciliation by painting a portrait of Tadeusz. She began work on the portrait towards the end of 1927, just before her husband set off on the fateful trip to Warsaw on which he was to meet the new love of his life and finally leave Lempicka. The portrait, mainly in shades of grey and black, shows an embittered man in a coat and scarf, as though about to leave. Red-rimmed eyes and a hardness about the mouth show nothing of the attractive *bon vivant* that the artist had once fallen in love with. She took her revenge at the humiliation of being abandoned by leaving the portrait unfinished: the left hand, on which he would have worn his wedding ring, was never completed.

Oil on canvas, 130 × 80.5 cm, Musée national d'art moderne, Paris

A 1987 article in the German news magazine *Der Spiegel* described Tamara de Lempicka as a "beautiful, man-eating butterfly" and wrote of her husband that "he lived as a person for twenty-five years and then as a husband for twelve years. After that, his soul was so distorted that he could barely open his mouth except to drink. Shortly before leaving France and his wife, he muttered, on the verge of madness: 'She is not a person. She is a monster'." [20]

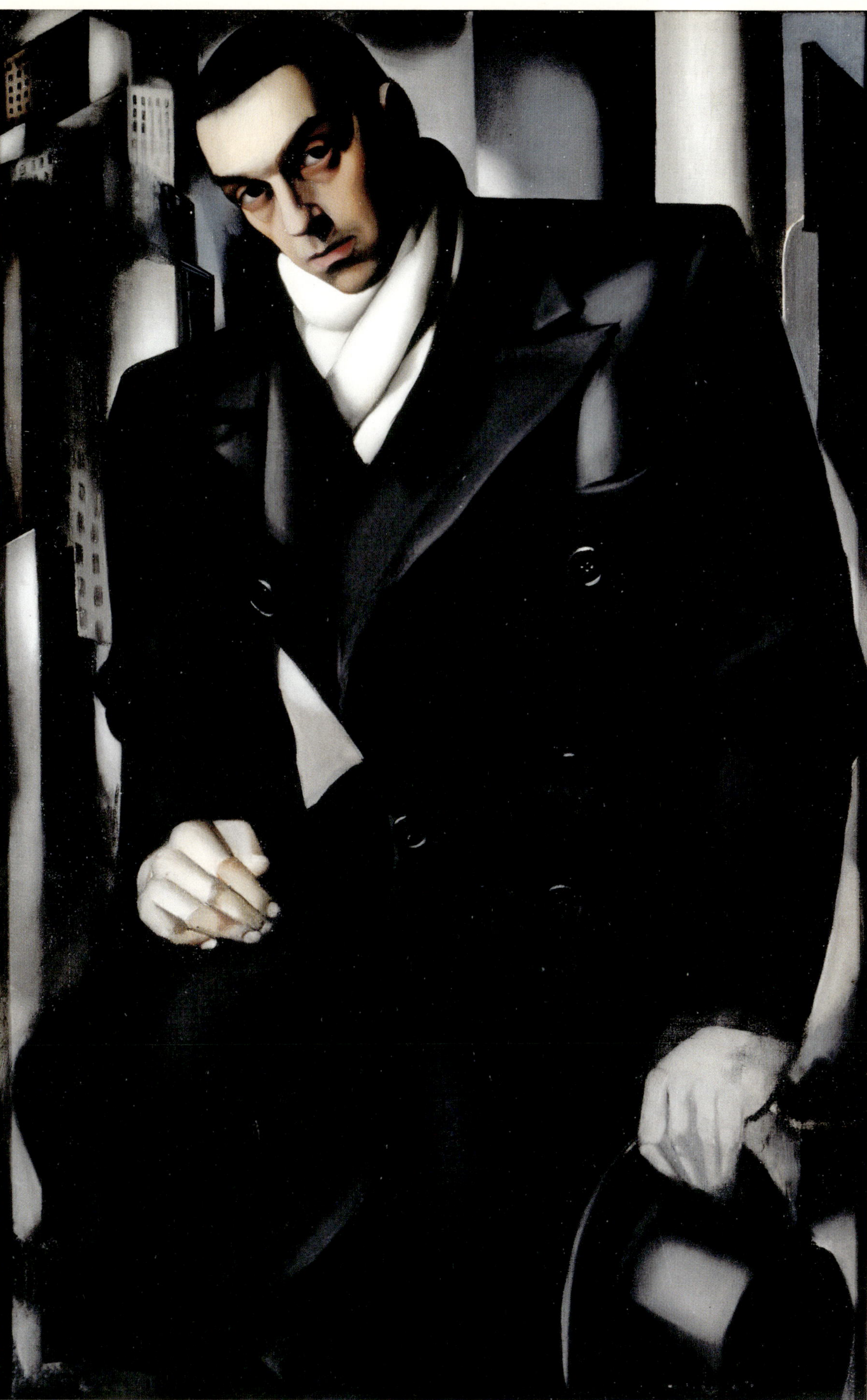

Lady in Blue with Guitar   1929

Oil on canvas, 116 × 75 cm,
private collection

"Whatever she painted had a metallic sheen, an icy
perfection that separated her objects from reality,
turning them into archetypes … Her Style was not
to conceal desire but to draw attention to it. The
coldness was part of the seduction." [21]

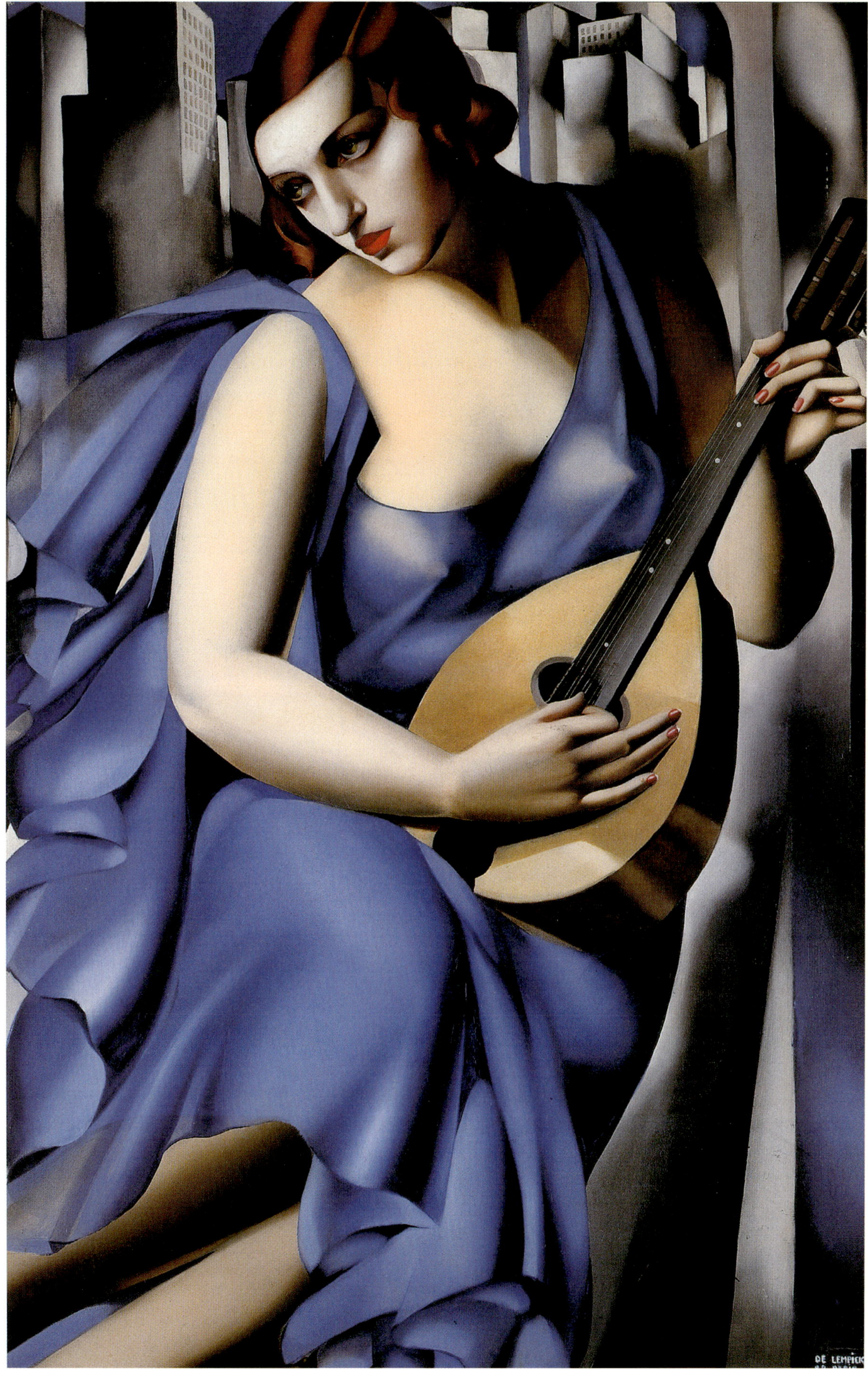

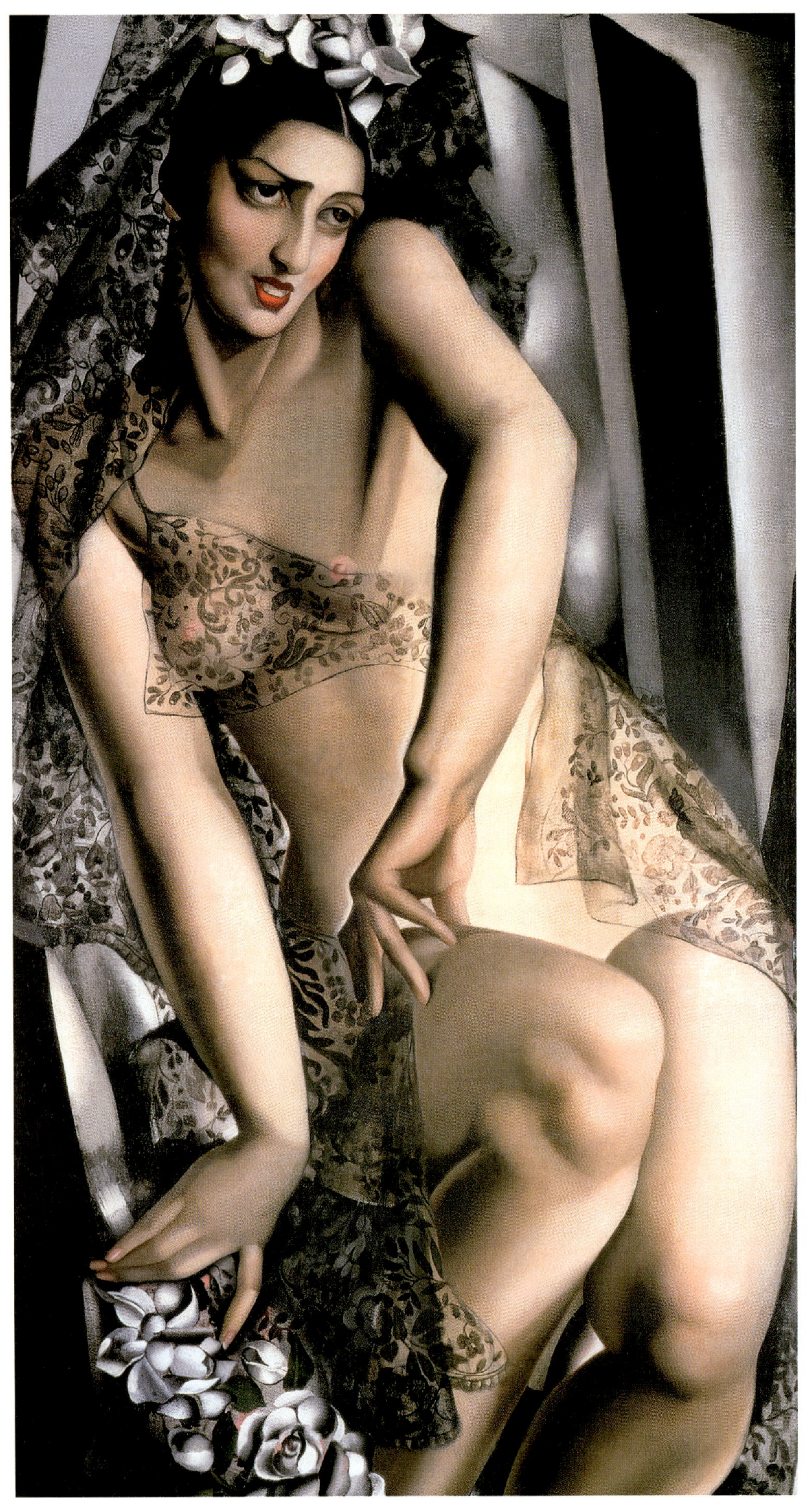

Oil on canvas, 121 × 64 cm,
private collection

Baron Raoul Kuffner's dark-haired mistress, the Andalusian
dancer Nana de Herrera, is wearing only the flimsiest piece of
chiffon whose function is not entirely clear. Her strangely distorted pose and somewhat pained expression reflect the
artist's reluctance to paint a flattering portrait of this woman.
"As long as she was dressed, it was impossible. So ugly. I
couldn't believe it. And I thought: 'This man has very bad
taste.' … And I was about to give up the portrait, not do it at
all, until I said: 'When you dance, how do you look?' And she
did this expression and I said: 'That's all right,' and then
I painted her."[22]

"Her fame as an artist is enshrouded in a veil of
scandal. That was a reflection of her character
and that was why she led an extraordinary life
and painted extraordinary pictures."[23]

Dr Boucard 1929
Arlette Boucard 1928
Madame Boucard 1931

Dr Boucard, a scientist who had made his fortune with a medicine called Lacteol, was to become one of Lempicka's most important patrons for a number of years. He commissioned portraits of himself, his wife and his daughter, and also bought various other paintings from the artist. This assured her of a life of relative ease.

In the full-length portrait Boucard is shown holding his invention in the form of a red liquid in a test tube, while grasping a microscope with his left hand. Here, Lempicka emphasises the professional qualifications of the sitter which determine the portrait like the insignia of power. The sitter is presented as a determined and resourceful man. The pose suggests movement, while the elegant coat is striking in its coolness of tone and the precision of its few folds.

The portrait of his wife, on the other hand, shows a melancholy, introspective lady in an evening dress with a wide décolleté, and a voluminous, red, fur-trimmed mantle draped over her shoulders. Her right shoulder is bare and the mantle seems to hover in the air above her left shoulder. Her earring, bracelet and ring underline her upper-class status. She is sitting in a rather vaguely defined pose and her feet (as in most of Lempicka's portraits) cannot be seen.

Portrait of Dr Boucard, 1929. Oil on canvas, 135 × 27 cm, private collection

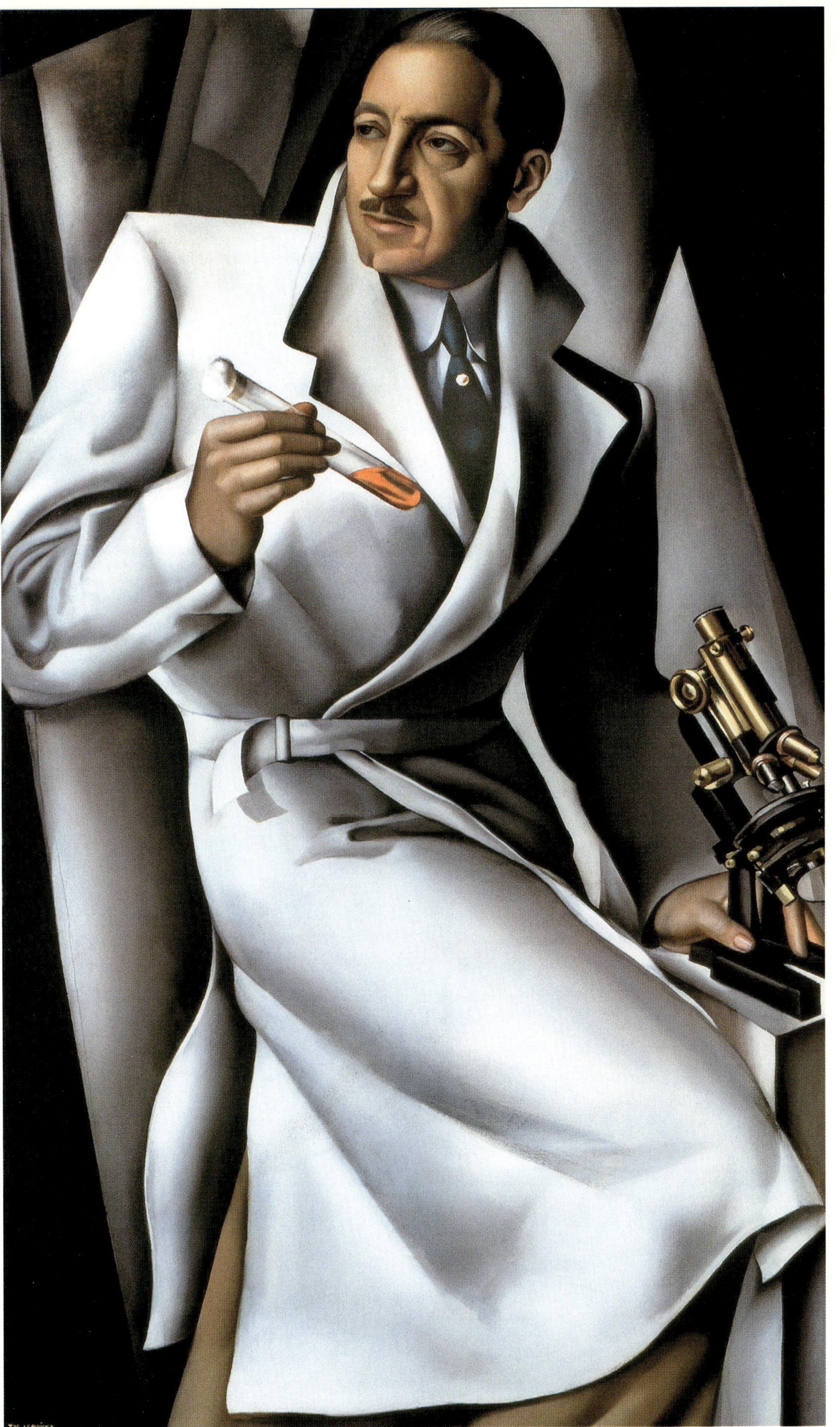

Portrait of Arlette Boucard,
1928. Oil on canvas,
70 × 130 cm, private collection

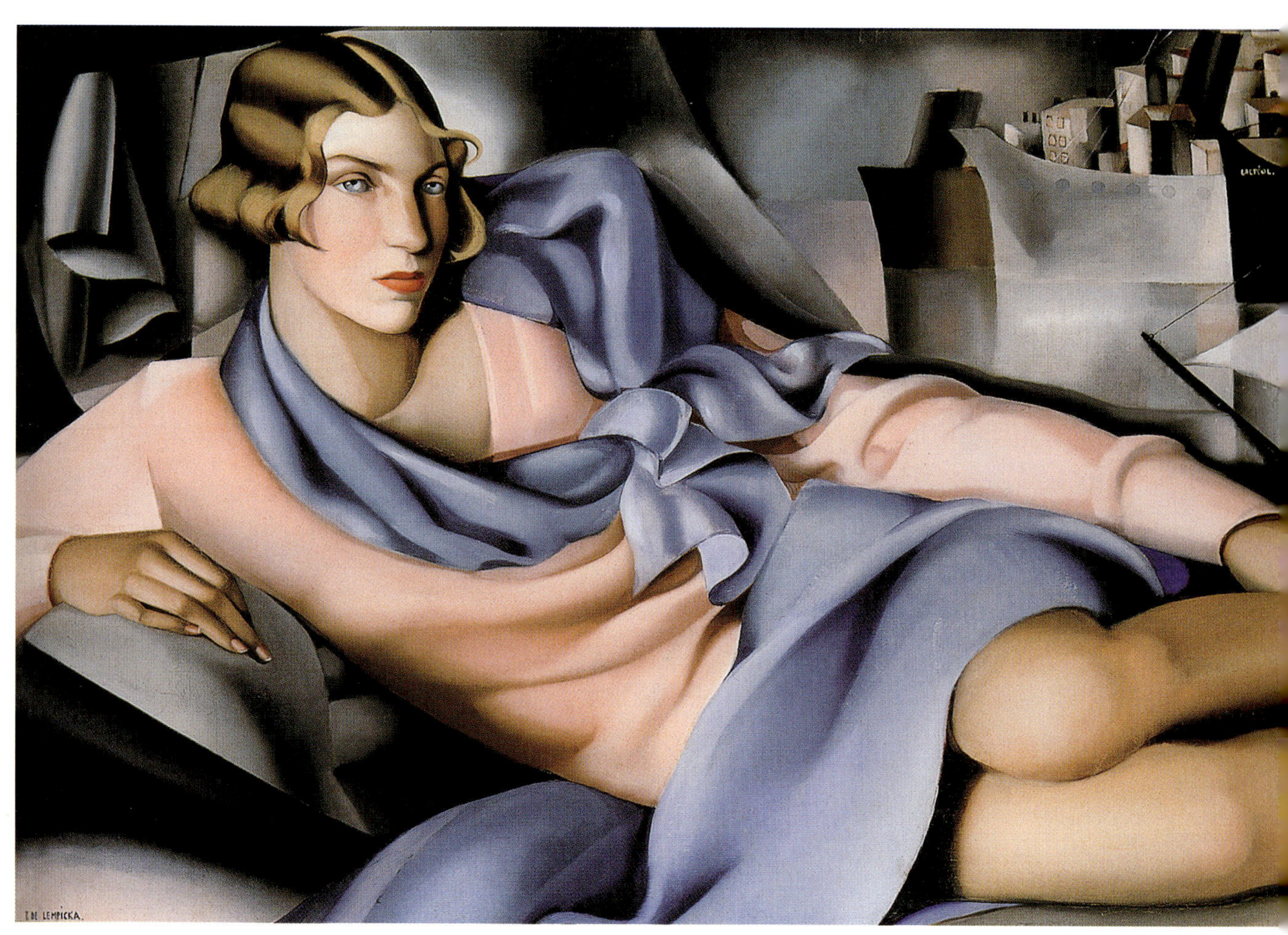

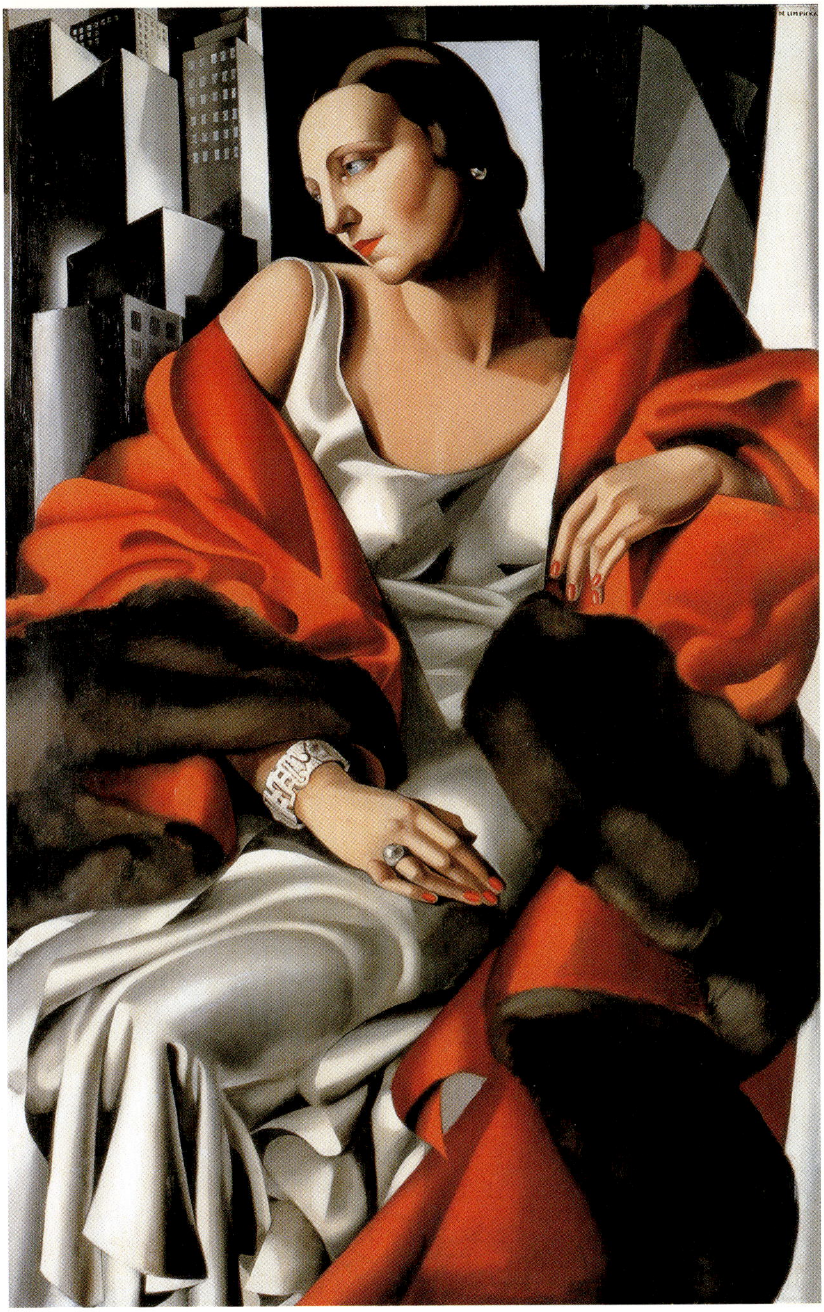

Portrait of Madame Boucard,
1931. Oil on wood,
135 × 75 cm, private collection

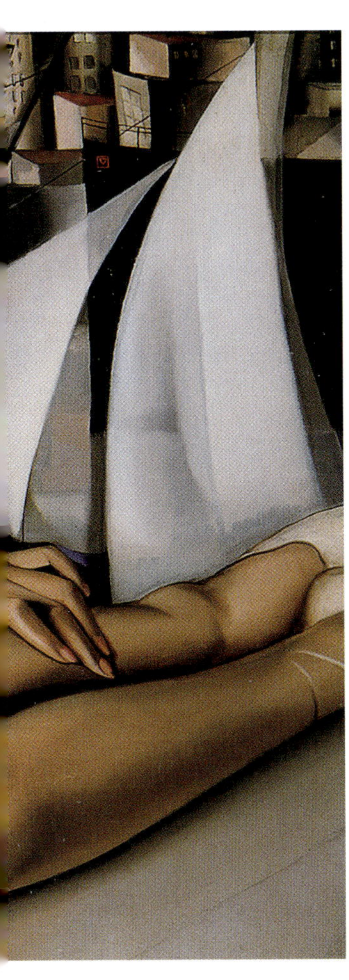

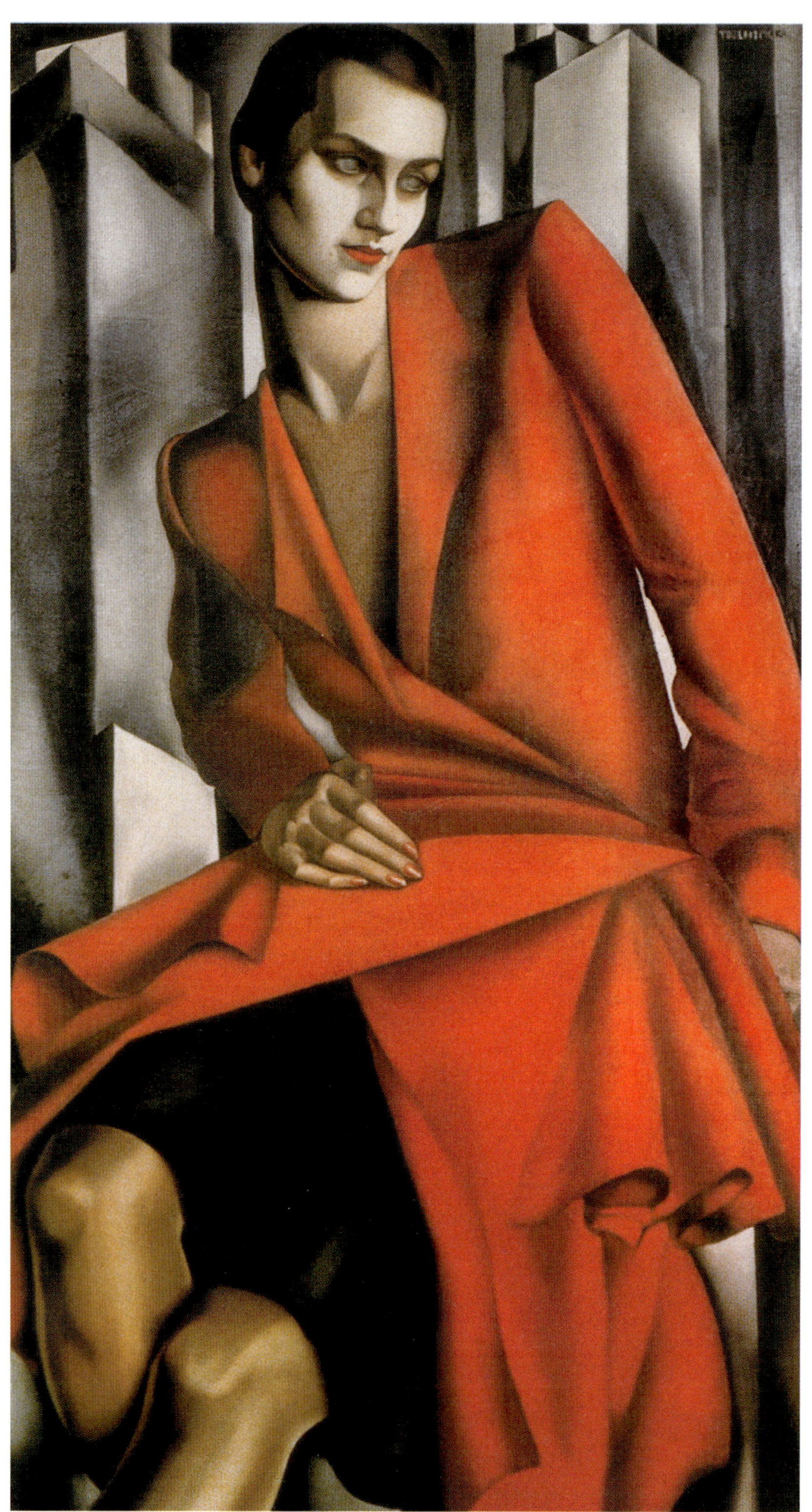

Oil on canvas, 122 × 66 cm,
private collection

Portrait of Mrs Bush   1929

In the late 1920s, Lempicka had the opportunity of travelling to America for the first time. She had been commissioned to go there to paint the portrait of the American millionaire Rufus Bush's fiancée. Bush not only unquestioningly accepted the fee she specified, but also, once she was there, met every request she made (regarding the sitter's clothes, the studio equipment etc.) without delay.

The Young Girls   1930

Oil on wood, 35 × 27 cm,
private collection

"In order to survive, I turned to painting. If my husband
had been a hard-working breadwinner, the artist Tamara
de Lempicka would never have seen the light of day."[24]

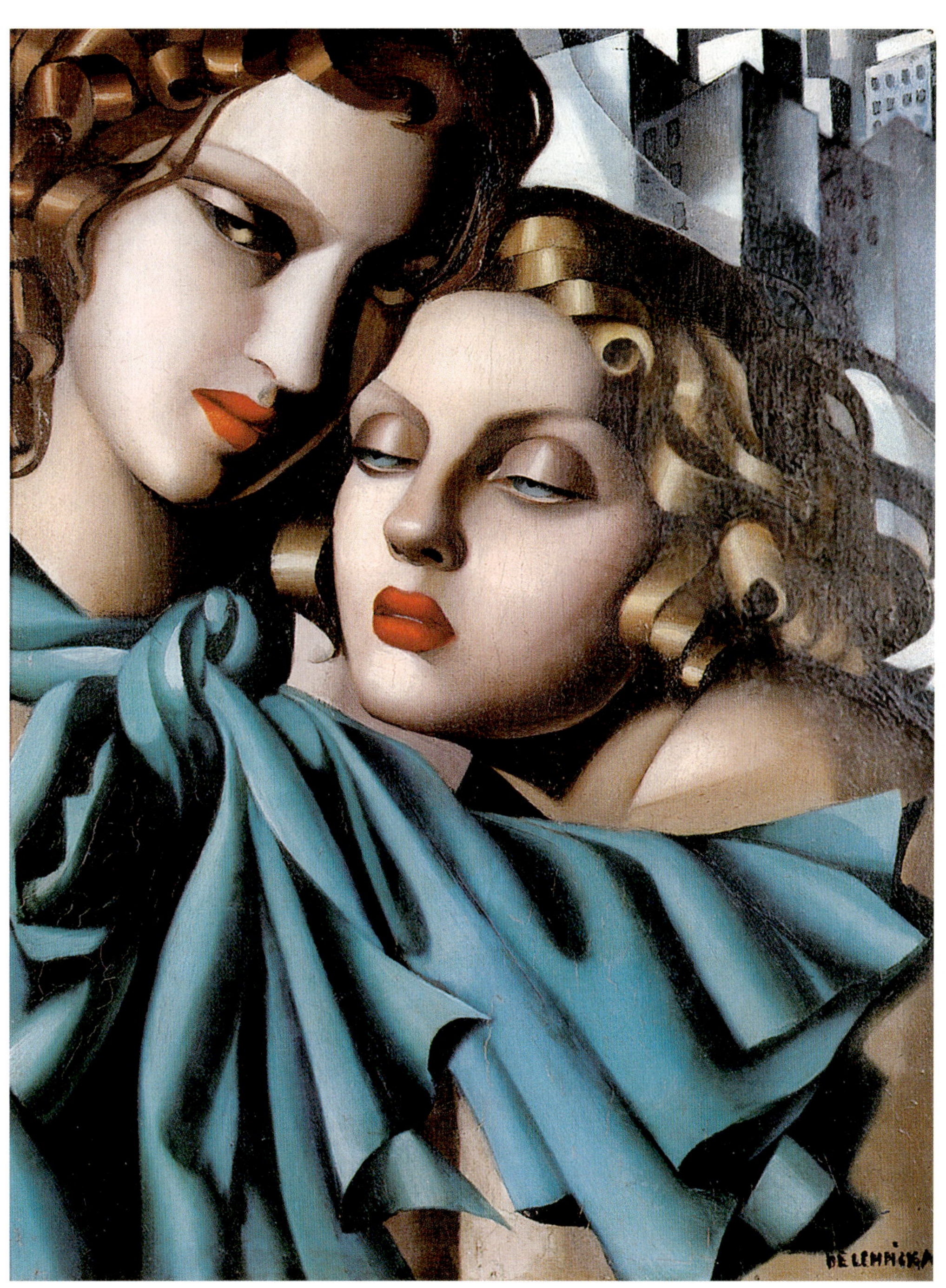

Women Bathing *c.* 1929

Seven naked women shamelessly flaunt their bodies in convoluted poses as they bathe, though bathing seems to be a secondary consideration here. The sometimes sketchy contours suggest that, for once, the artist has not pursued the metallic coldness that is the hallmark of most of her other paintings. The right arm of the woman reclining in the foreground even seems unfinished. The group composition is clearly inspired by Ingres's *Turkish Bath*. Critics immediately accused her of 'perverse Ingrism' which ensured her invaluable publicity.

Oil on canvas, dimensions unknown, private collection

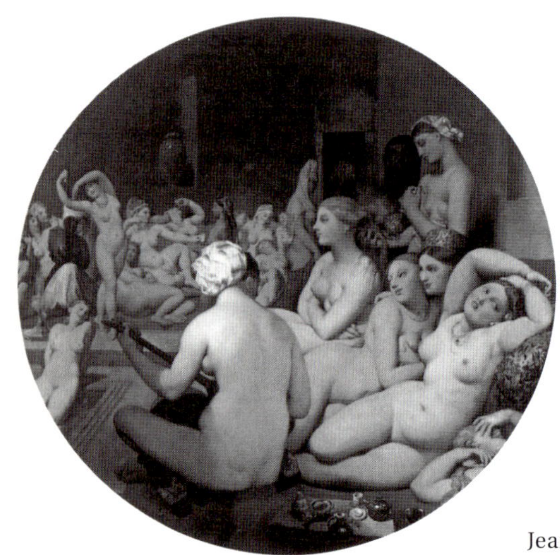

Jean Auguste Dominique Ingres, *Turkish Bath*, 1862. Oil on canvas, mounted on wood, diameter 108 cm, Musée du Louvre, Paris

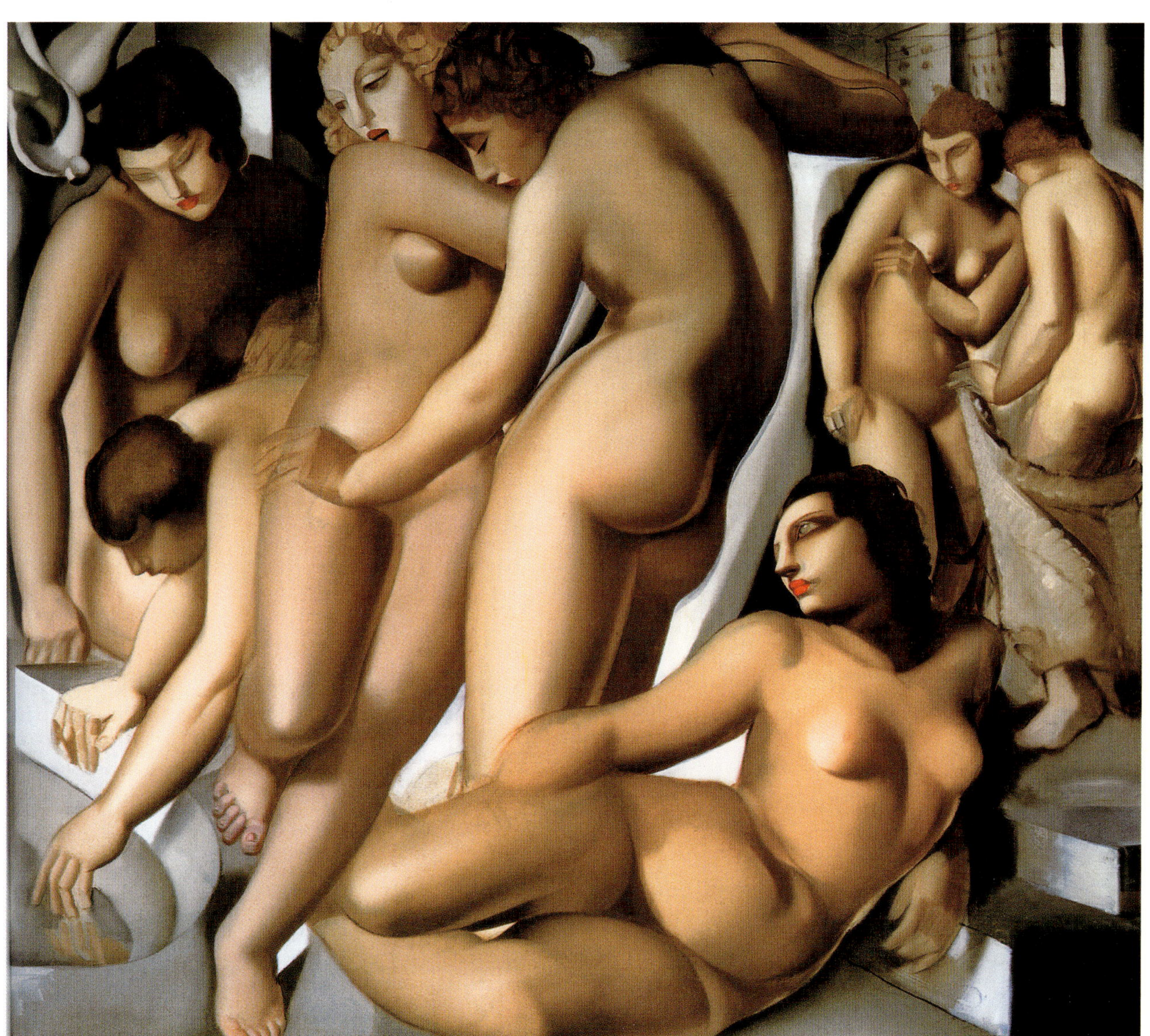

Adam and Eve   1932

One of the anecdotes the artist loved to tell was of the time she was working with a professional model who asked if she could eat an apple during her break. She was still naked. "I had an inspiration. … I called quickly: 'Stop! You must hold that pose exactly as it is. Don't move'. And I sketched furiously. I knew that in that moment that what I saw was Eve and that I must find my Adam. When I finished the sketch, I went out into the streets. This was the artists' quarter. I had before me the vision of Adam and Eve. In the street nearby I saw a gendarme, a policeman on his beat. He was young, he was handsome. I said to him: 'Monsieur, I am an artist and I need a model for my painting. Would you pose for me?' And he said: 'Of course, Madame. I am myself an artist. At what time do you require me?' … He came to my studio after work and said: 'How shall I pose?' 'In the nude'. He took off his things and folded them neatly on the chair, placing his big revolver on the top. I set him on the podium and then called my model. 'You are Adam and here is your Eve', I said."[25] The two nudes have an almost statuesque pose, seemingly constrained by the picture format, the head and feet cropped, as in so many of her paintings. The eyes without pupils emphasise the stone-like character of Adam and Eve, who seem to be frozen in this pose. The immaculate nudity is accentuated only by heavy shadows that form a continuation of the geometric urban architectural elements in the background. What is particularly interesting here is the fact that the male nude seems to dominate the picture. It is as though his body has been modelled with devotion, while the female nude is very much in the background.

The price of two million dollars paid for this painting in 1994 revived the old debate about the true value of a work of art or its author once again. In the Thirties, Lempicka had tried in vain to sell this painting for 15,000 francs – equivalent to about 20,000 dollars today.

Oil on cardboard, 118 × 74 cm, Musée d'art moderne, Petit Palais, Geneva

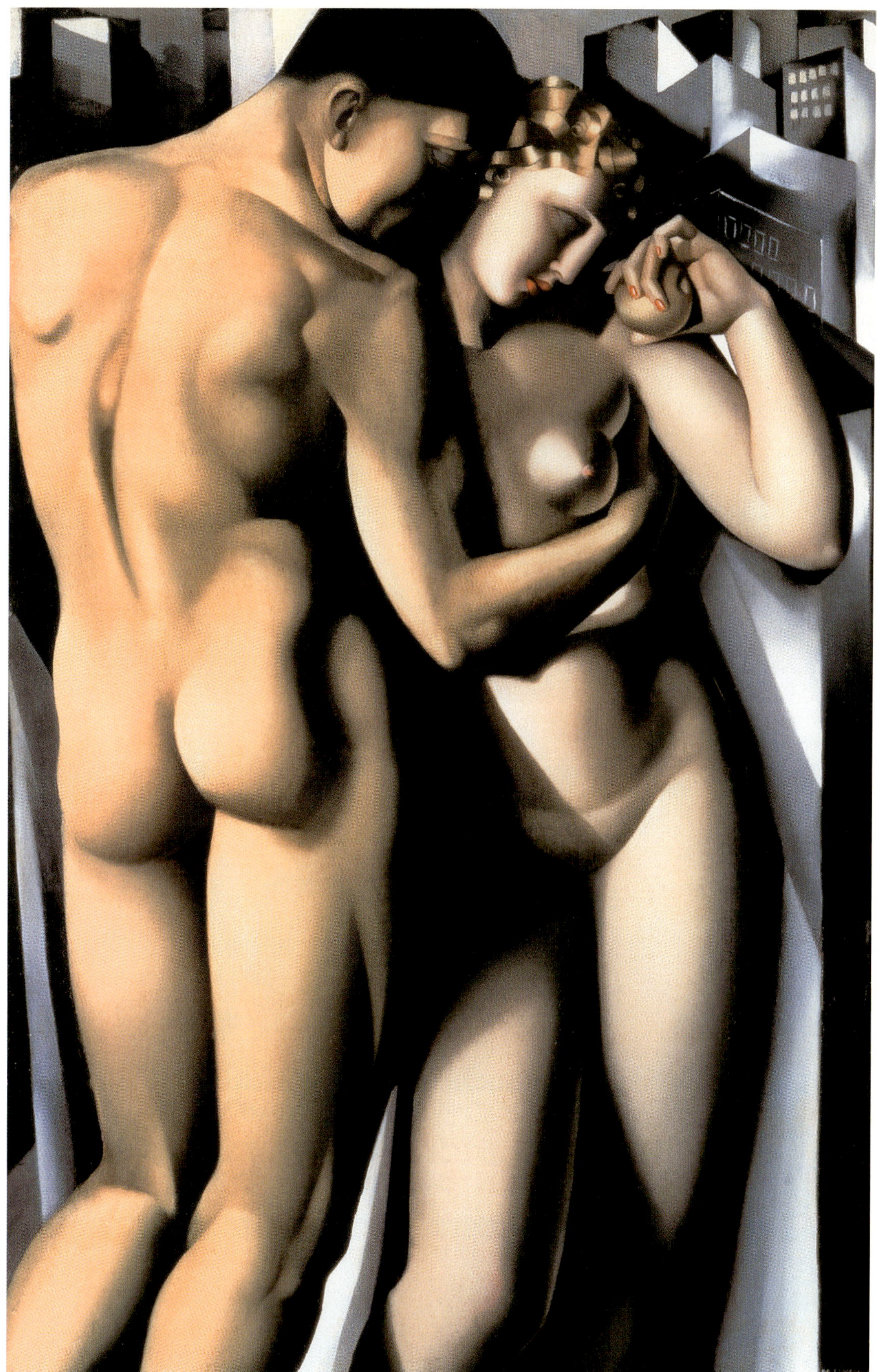

Calla Lilies   1931

Oil on wood, 55 × 33 cm,
private collection

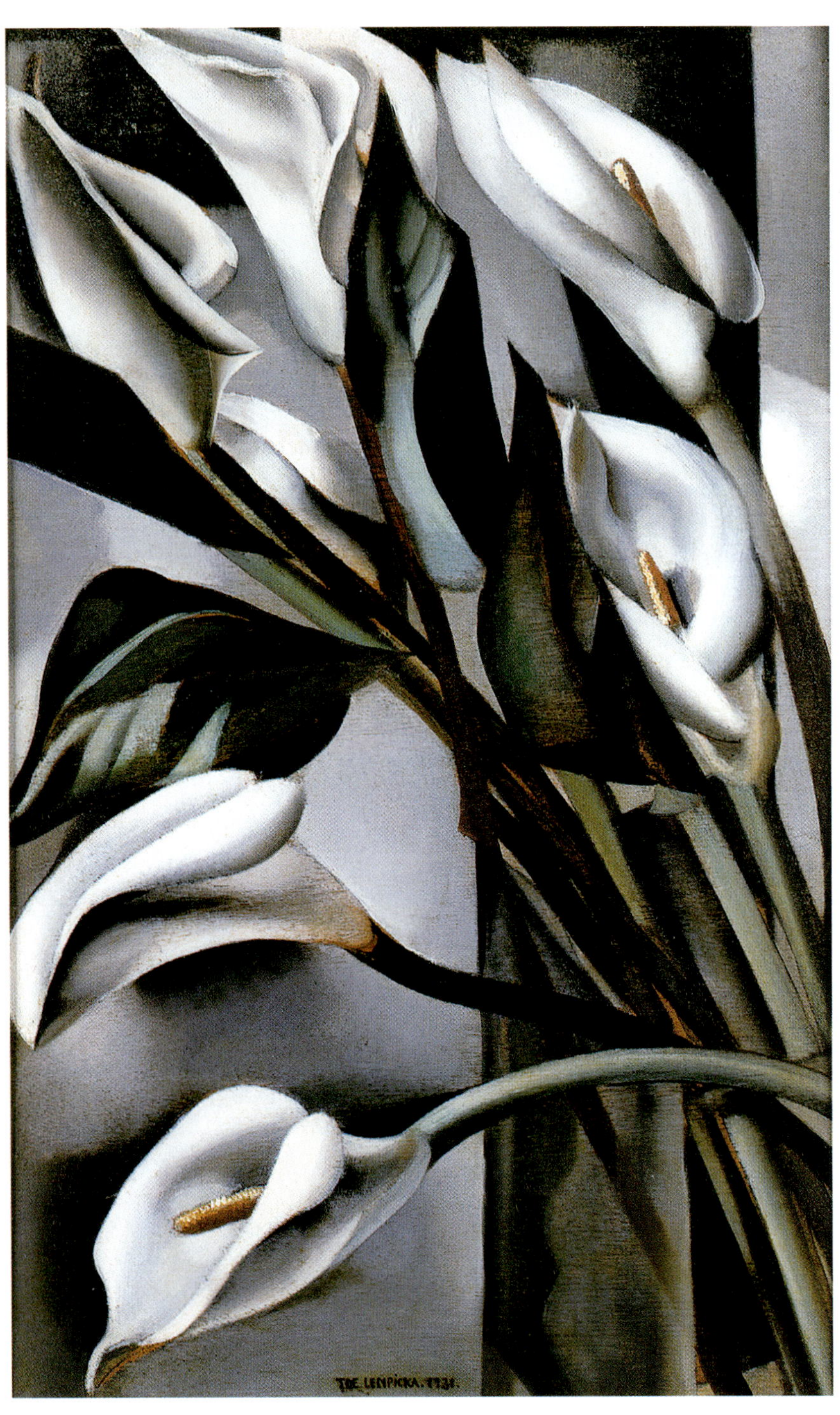

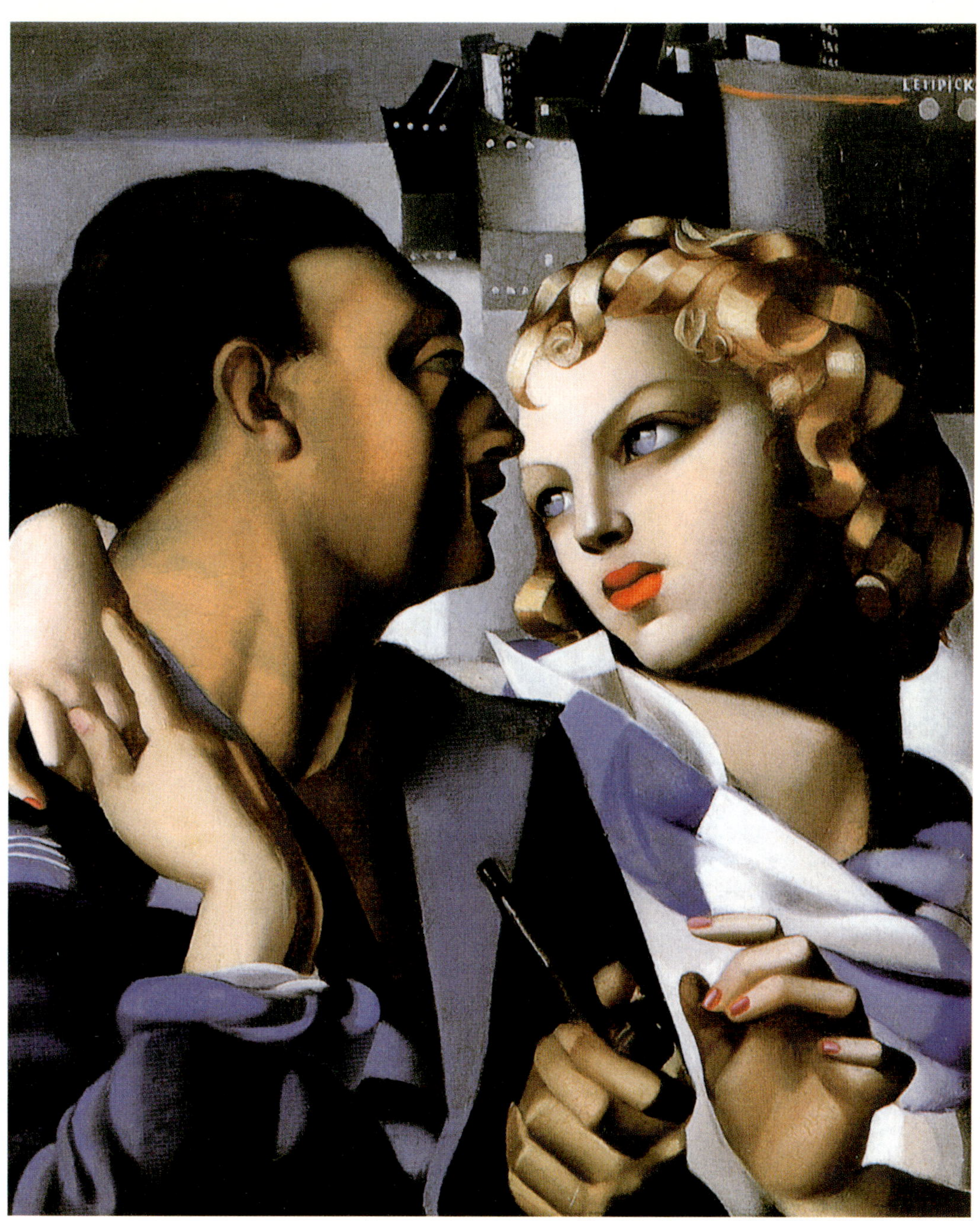

Idyll 1931

Oil on canvas, 45 × 35 cm,
private collection

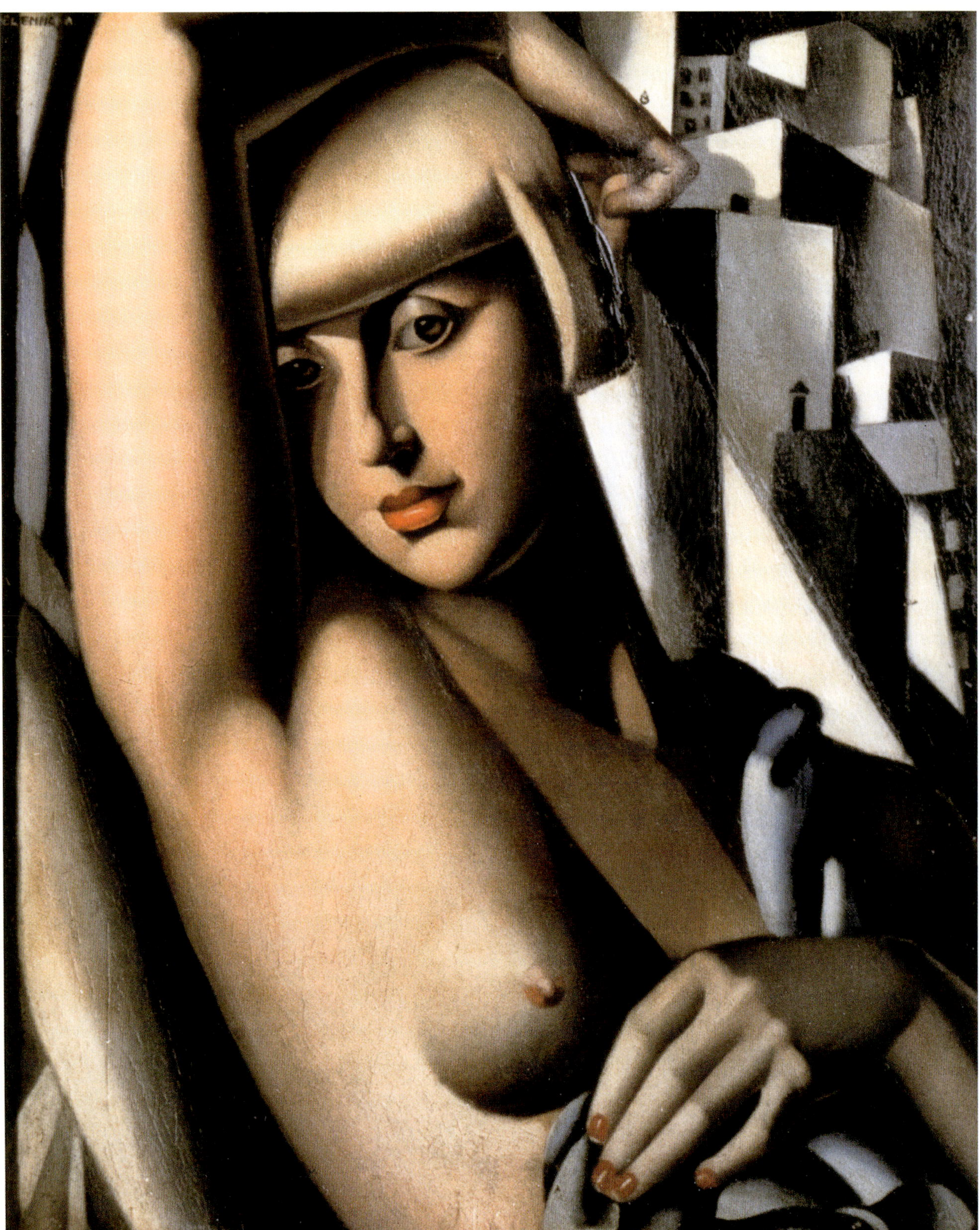

Portrait of Suzy Solidor 1933

Born in the town of Deauville in the north of France, Suzy Rocher changed her name to Suzy Solidor when she arrived in Paris in the late Twenties. She began a career as a singer and by 1930 had opened her own nightclub 'Boite de Nuit'.

One of her most famous publicity moves was to become the 'world's most frequently painted woman'. She sat for the leading artists of the day, including Picasso and Georges Braque. All she asked in return was that she be allowed to exhibit the painting in her nightclub. By the early Thirties, there were no fewer than thirty-three portraits of her on the walls. With that, 'Boite de Nuit' became one of the trendiest places in Paris.

Solidor met Lempicka several times and also asked her if she would paint her portrait. Lempicka agreed, but only on condition that she could paint her nude.

**Sleeping Girl
(Kizette) I**   *c.* 1933

Oil on wood, 31 × 41 cm,
private collection

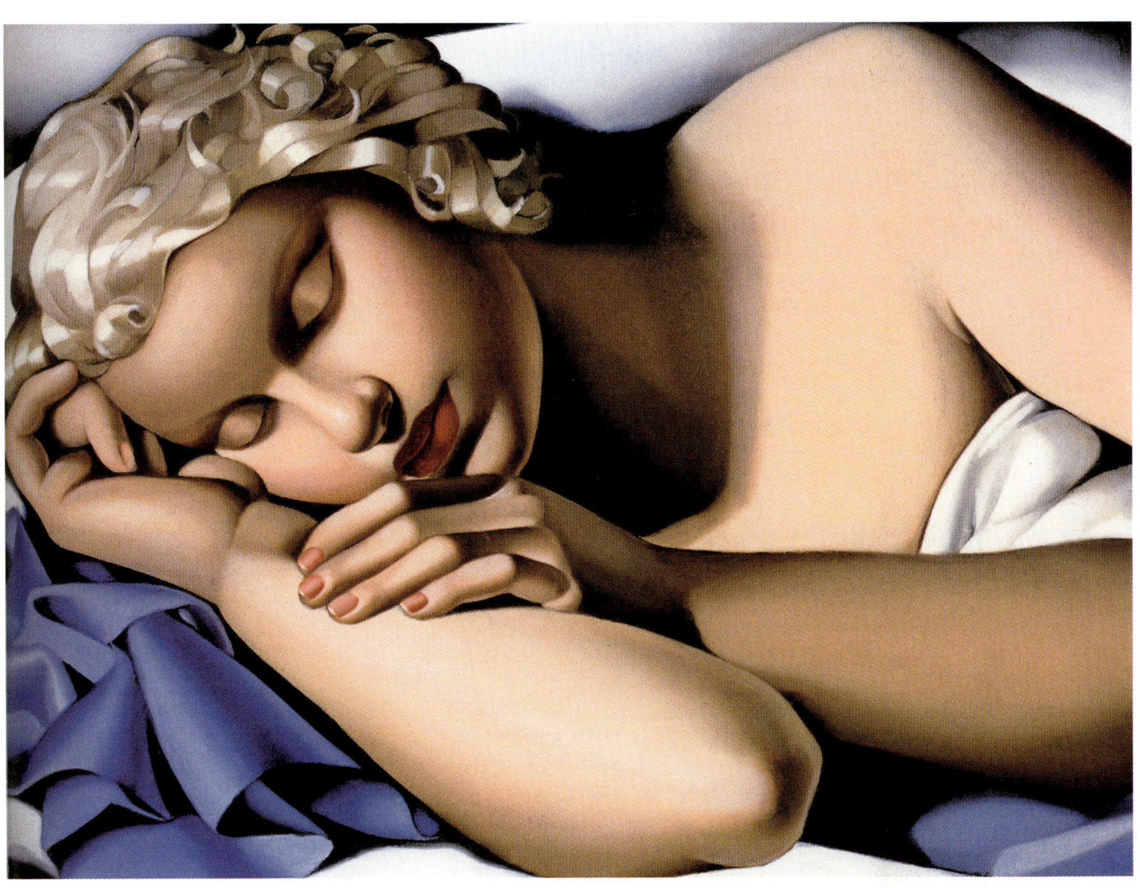

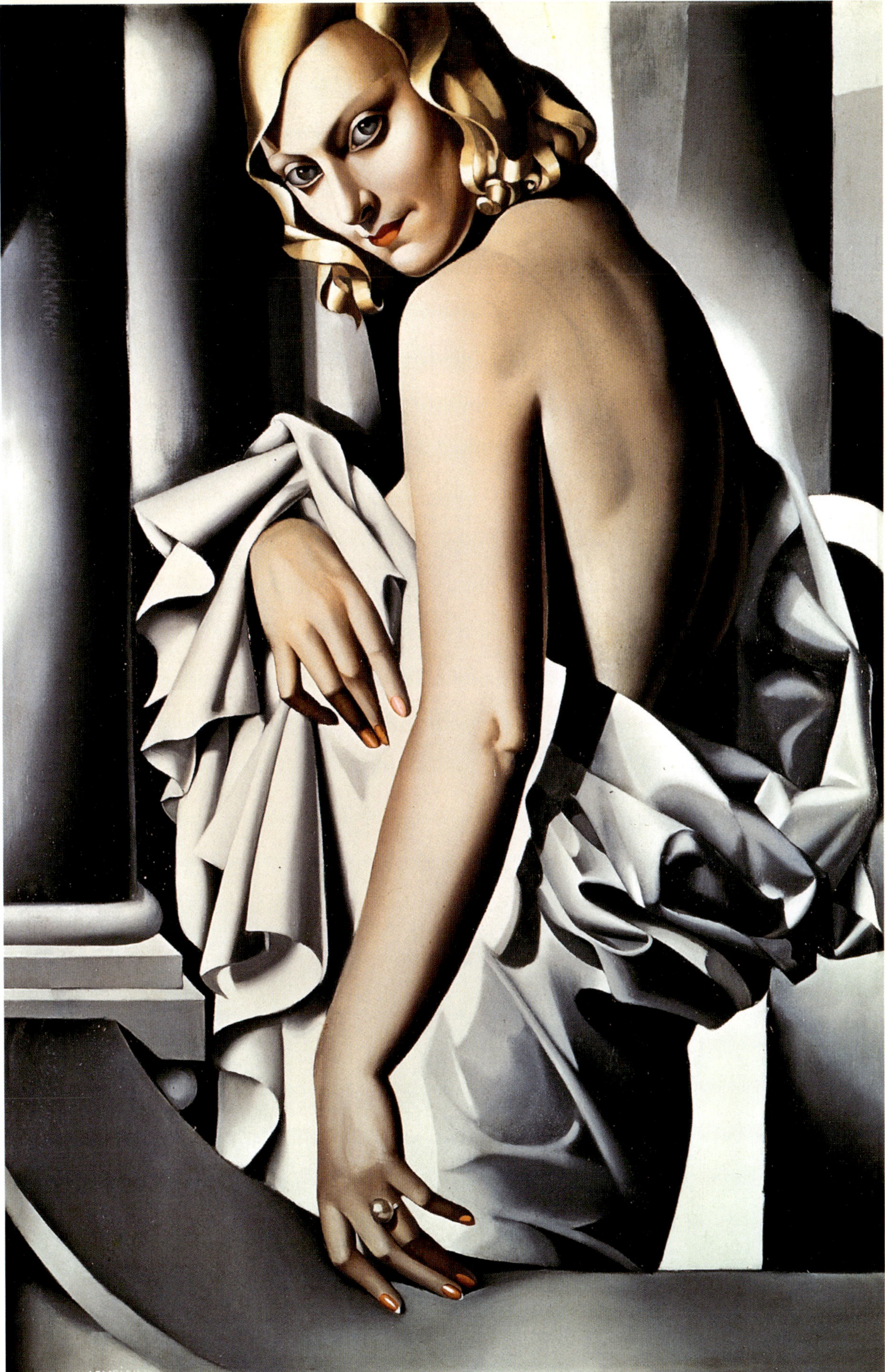
LEMPICKA

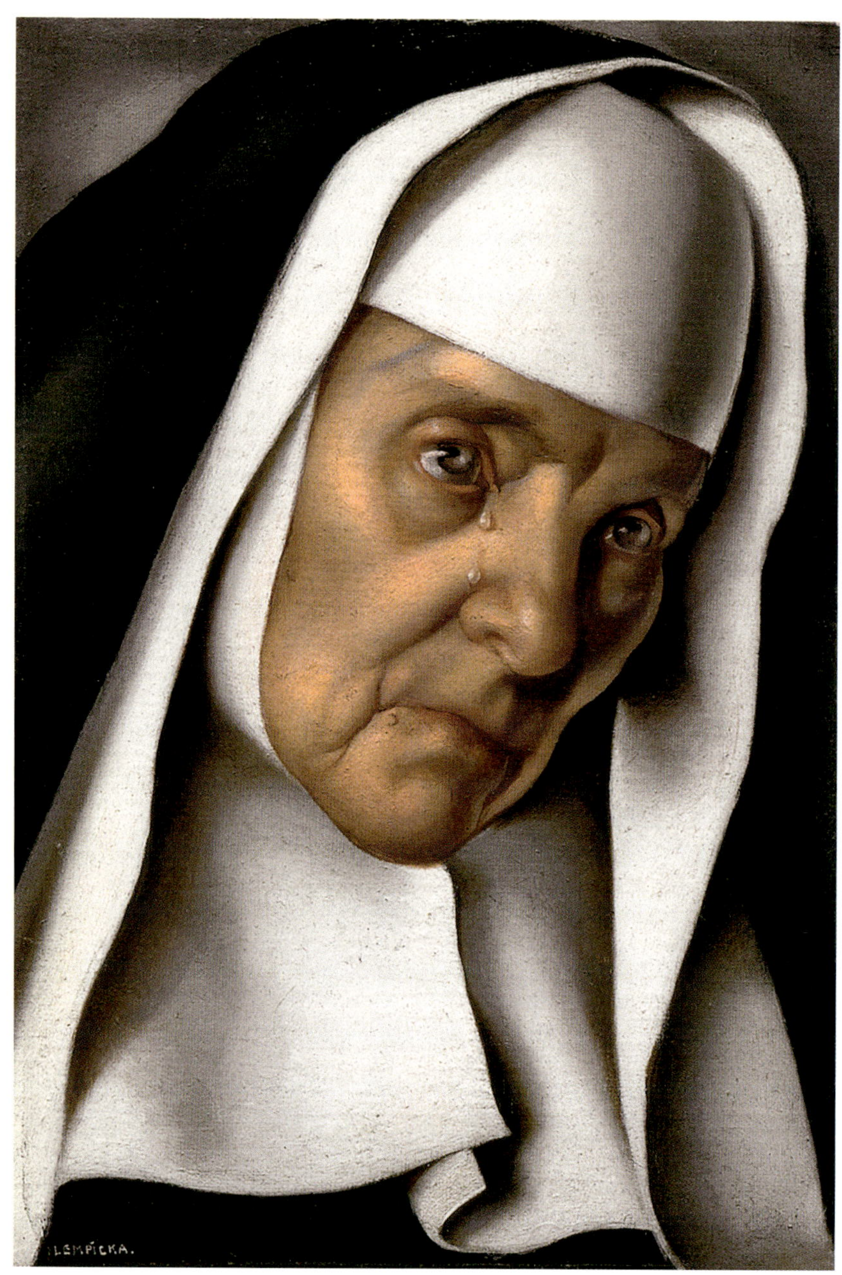

Mother Superior   1935

Oil on canvas, 30 × 20 cm,
Musée des Beaux-Arts, Nantes

Old Man with a Guitar
(Beggar with Mandolin)   1935

Oil on canvas, 66 × 50 cm,
Musée Departement de l'Oise,
Beauvais

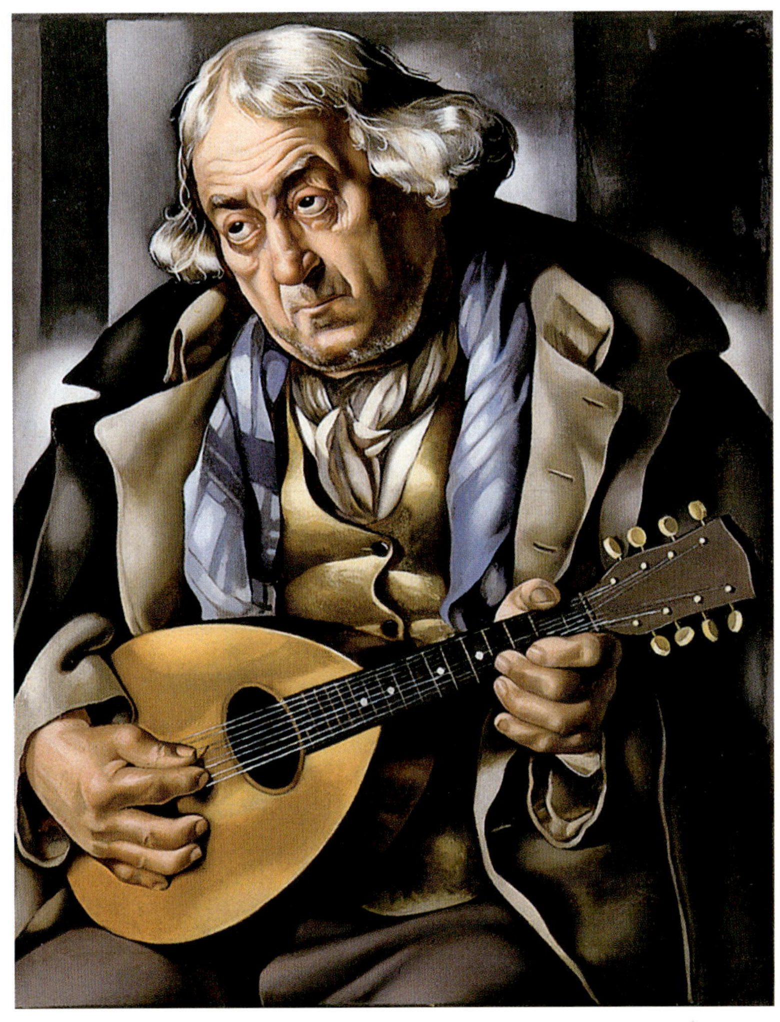

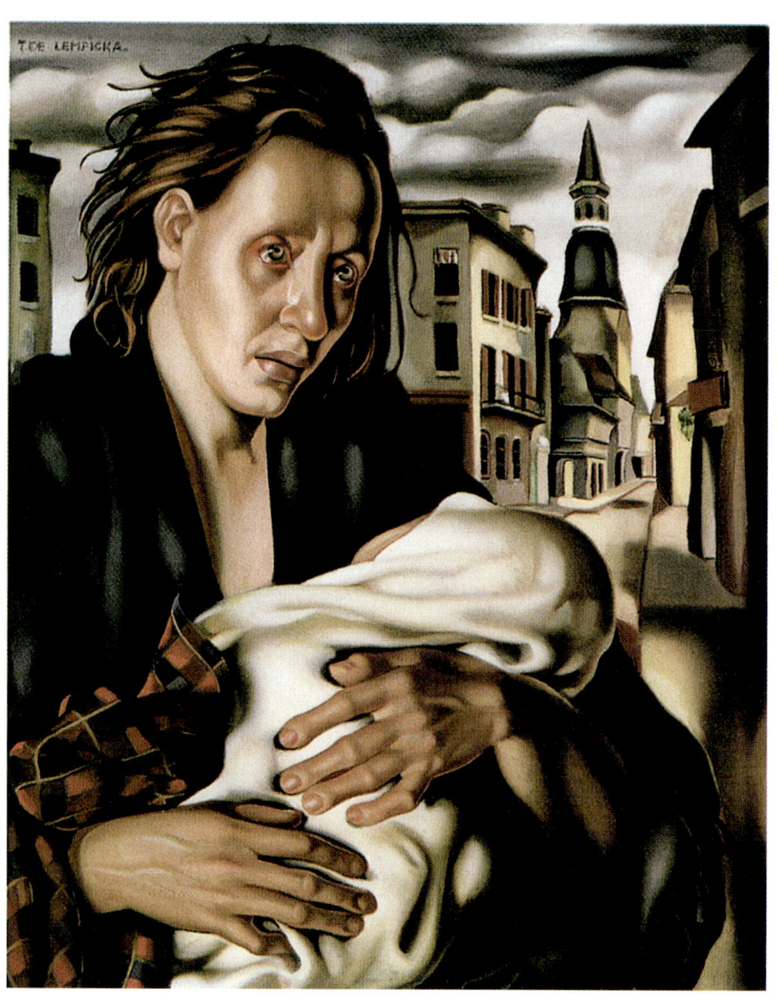

Flight   1940

Oil on canvas, 50.8 × 40.6 cm,
Musée des Beaux-Arts, Nantes

Autumn   1953

Oil on canvas,
86.5 × 106.5 cm,
private collection

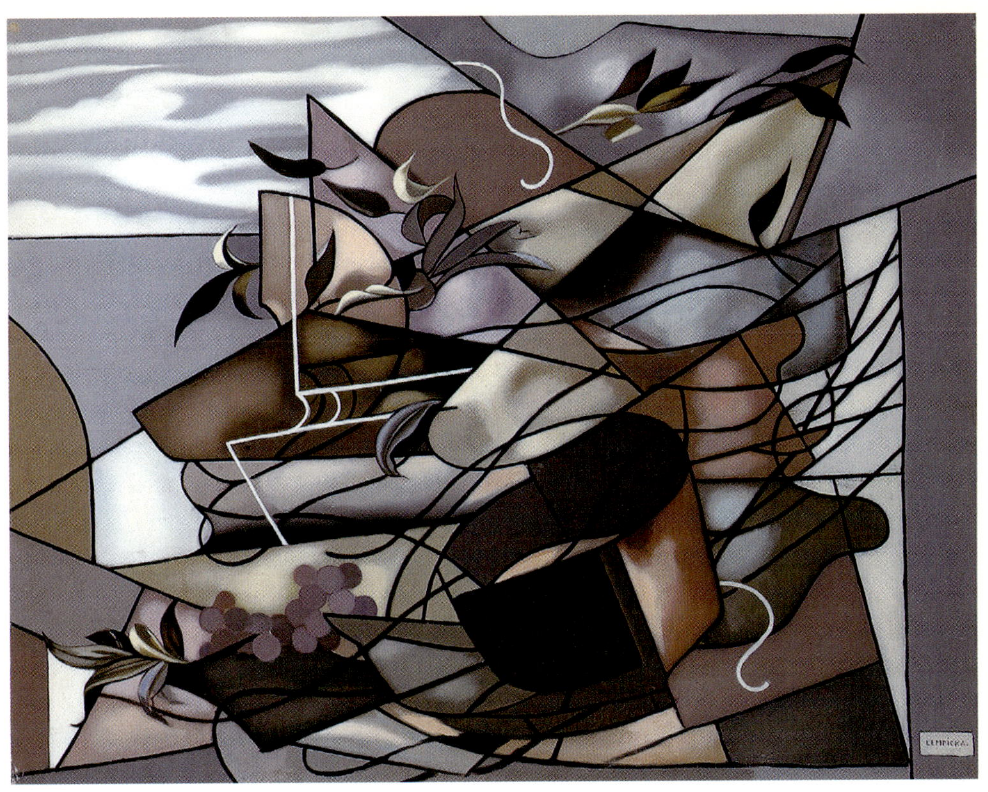

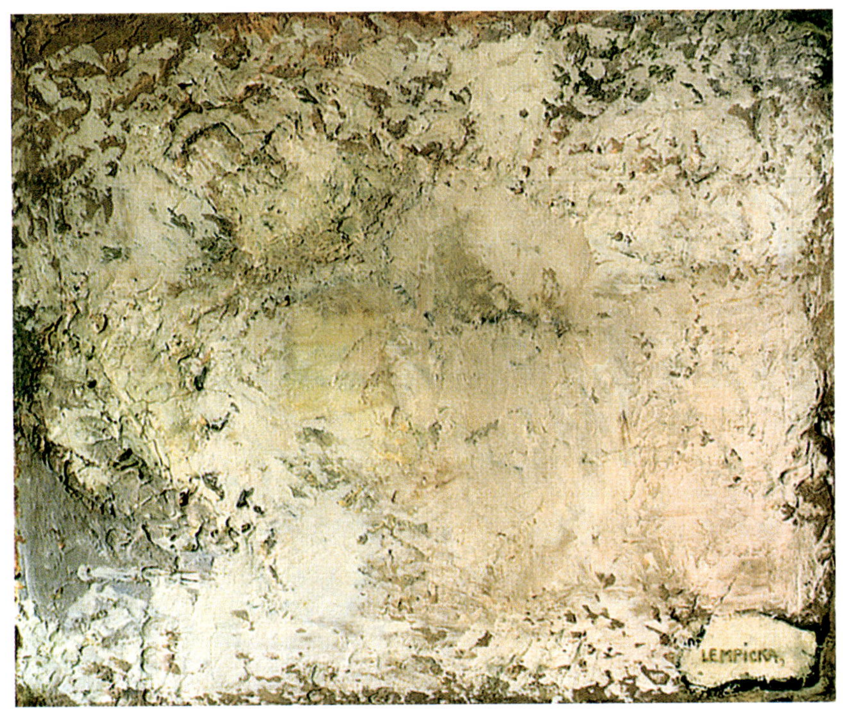

**Abstract Composition
in White**   *c.* 1959

Oil on canvas, 30.5 × 35.5 cm,
Succession Lempicka

ENDNOTES

1   Wieland Schmied (ed.), *Der Kühle Blick*, Munich 2001, p. 34
2   Kizette de Lempicka-Foxhall, *Passion by Design, The Art and Times of Tamara de Lempicka*, New York 1987, pp. 52–53
3   Jean Clair, 'Vom Roten Oktober zum Schwarzen Oktober' in *Der Kühle Blick*, ed. Wieland Schmied, op. cit., p. 37. [Essay originally published in French: Jean Clair, 'De l'octobre rouge à l'octobre noir', in *Les Années 20: l'âge des métropoles*, Montreal 1991, pp. 17–41]
4   Laura Claridge, *Tamara de Lempicka, A Life of Deco and Decadence*, New York 1999, pp. 71–72.
5   Tamara de Lempicka 1979, in Masuda/Ishioka 1980, p. 24, cited by Thormann, op. cit., p. 123
6   Wieland Schmied, 'Der kühle Blick', in *Der Kühle Blick*, op. cit., p. 12
7   Kizette de Lempicka-Foxhall, op. cit., p. 66
8   Kizette de Lempicka-Foxhall, op. cit., p. 90
9   Lempicka to Tadeusz in her hotel in Italy, cited by Laura Claridge, op. cit., p. 145
10   Kizette de Lempicka-Foxhall, op. cit., p. 96
11   Franco Maria Ricci, *Tamara de Lempicka*, Parma 1977, p. 24
12   Kizette de Lempicka-Foxhall, op. cit., pp. 58–59
13   Curt Moreck, *Das Weib in der Kunst der neueren Zeit*, Berlin 1925, pp. 384–85, citing Thormann, op. cit., p. 137
14   Lempicka, in Alain Blondel, *Tamara de Lempicka*, catalogue raisonné 1921–1979, Lausanne 1999, p. 79
15   Kizette de Lempicka-Foxhall, op. cit., p. 43
16   Kizette de Lempicka-Foxhall, op. cit., p. 53
17   Lempicka, cited by Kizette de Lempicka-Foxhall, op. cit., p. 76
18   Kizette de Lempicka-Foxhall, op. cit., p. 43
19   Kizette de Lempicka-Foxhall, op. cit., p. 172
20   *Der Spiegel* No. 45, 2.11.1987, p. 251, citing Thormann, op. cit., p. 166
21   Kizette de Lempicka-Foxhall, op. cit., p. 84
22   Lempicka, cited by Kizette de Lempicka-Foxhall, op. cit., p. 94
23   Kizette de Lempicka-Foxhall, op. cit., p. 17
24   Tamara de Lempicka 1979, in Eiko Ishioka, *Tamara de Lempicka, die Frau mit den stählernen Pupillen*, in Masuda/Ishioka 1980, p. 25, cited by Ellen Thormann, *Kunstkritik und Künstlerinnen in Paris*, Berlin 1993, p. 120
25   Lempicka, cited by Kizette de Lempicka-Foxhall, op. cit., p. 82

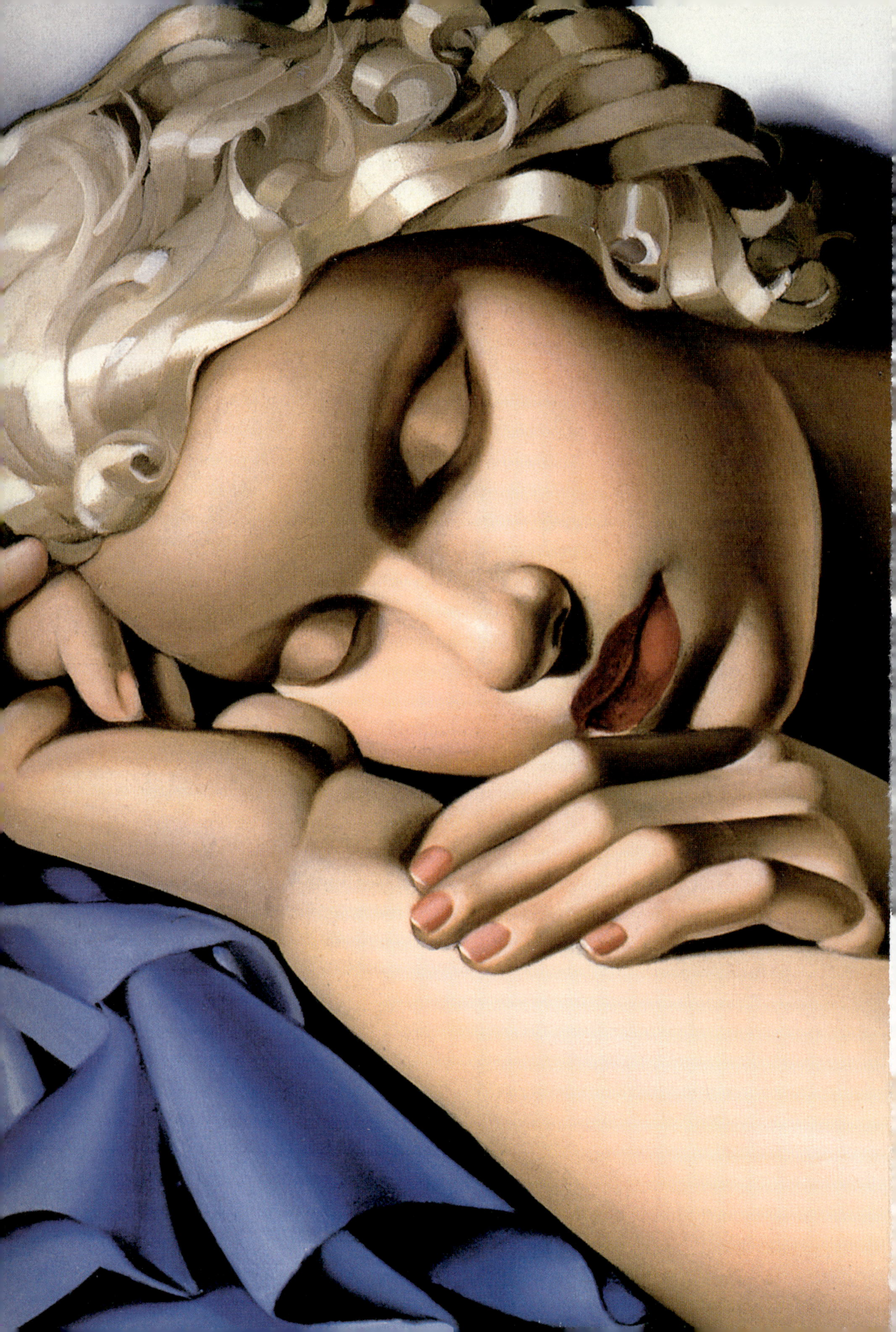